122 Clues For Jews
Whose Children Intermarry

D1474853

122 Clues for Jews Whose Children Intermarry

Sidney J. Jacobs, M.A.H.L., D.D.
Betty J. Jacobs, M.A.

JACOBS LADDER PUBLICATIONS
Culver City, California

First Edition

Copyright © 1988 by
Sidney J. Jacobs and Betty J. Jacobs

All rights reserved. No part of this book
may be reproduced, stored in a retrieval system or
transmitted, in any form or by any means, without prior
written permission from the authors or publisher.

Library of Congress Catalog Card Number 87-83147
ISBN 0-933647-01-8

Printed in the United States of America
9 8 7 6 5 4 3 2 1

To
Sid's parents, Emanuel and Sarah Jacobs, of blessed memory,
and Betty's parents, Saul and Rae Lazaroff

and to
the children:
Aviva, Jonathan, Michael, Nehama and Stefanie

Contents

About the Authors

Sidney J. Jacobs, M.A.H.L., D.D., is an ordained rabbi and journalist. A valedictory graduate of Northwestern University's Medill School of Journalism, he began his professional writing career at the Chicago City News Bureau and went on to become an editor in Chicago and Los Angeles. He received his rabbinical ordination from Rabbi Stephen S. Wise at the Hebrew Union College—Jewish Institute of Religion. Rabbi Jacobs has led congregations in Illinois, Minnesota and California. In his work as a rabbi, journalist and social activist, he has encountered hundreds of intermarried couples and their families. He is the author of *The Jewish Word Book* (1982) and co-author of *Clues About Jews For People Who Aren't* (1985).

Betty J. Jacobs, M.A., is a professor of communications at West Los Angeles College in California. She is a media consultant and free-lance writer who has been the recipient of awards for television writing and production and who has created special media projects for the California Consortium of Community Colleges. She served as director of broadcasting for the Chicago Board of Rabbis and has produced more than 600 television programs of Jewish content. In addition to the present volume, she is the co-author of *Clues About Jews For People Who Aren't* (1985).

Rabbi Sid and Betty live in Culver City, California (on the old MGM Lot #3) with their two dogs, Adam Randolph and Dodi-Li Daniel, and with the latest addition to the family, Carlyle, a well-tempered computer.

Authors' Note

The situations described in this book are real. Names and other details, such as occupations, have been changed to avoid recognition of the individuals involved. No identification with actual persons is intended or should be inferred.

Introduction

This book is a "how-to," a guidebook to the day-to-day problems that perplex and pain the Jewish parents of intermarried or about-to-be intermarried children. We offer it to you who seek advice and support in coping with your feelings and reactions to the new experiences that come with the intermarriage of your child: wedding plans, holidays, relationships with the in-laws, dealing with your grandchildren, Jewish identity, among other baffling situations.

The tremendous increase in marriages between American Jews and persons who are not is regarded by seasoned observers of the contemporary Jewish scene as one of the most significant developments in modern Jewish history.

Such unions are customarily called "intermarriages," less frequently "mixed marriages." Both terms designate marriages between men and women of differing religious, racial or ethnic backgrounds. When we write about a marital or pre-marital situation involving a Jew and a person of another religion, we have in mind a non-Jew who has not been converted to Judaism. The marriage of a Jew and a convert to Judaism is simply a union between two Jews, nothing less.

The writing of a book such as this would have been improbable 50 years ago. Intermarriage was a relatively infrequent occurrence and posed little threat to the integrity and survival of the Jewish group. Even further back in Jewish history, when a Jew married "out of the faith," the event was often accompanied by his or her assuming the religion of the non-Jewish spouse and abdicating the Jewish fold, since civil marriages were a rarity in the European community compared with unions blessed by the church.

The circumstances have changed dramatically and, for concerned Jews, traumatically, in the last few decades. The rate of intermarriage between Jews and non-Jews in the United States has tripled and quadrupled since World War II. The "guesstimate" is that 30 to

40 percent of Jews who marry today marry partners who are not Jewish.

The reasons why the statistics have gone berserk are not arcane. The social structure has changed dramatically, especially in the large urban centers of this country where the preponderance of American Jews live. No longer are we confined to ghettos where we live, where we work, where we study, where we play. The "five o'clock shadow" which used to divide Jews in the United States from their Gentile associates at the end of a work day has vanished.

Most significant, the singles bar is not segregated; neither is the aerobics class, the vacation cruise nor the campus. What the academics have described by the intimidating term of "social mobility" is now full-blown; and when social mobility has come, can intermarriage be far behind?

As deeply committed Jews, we are dismayed at the gradual attrition of Jewish ranks by astronomical rates of intermarriage. However, instead of wringing our hands or donning sackcloth and ashes or medieval garb and retreating into self-segregating Jewish ghettos in New York, Los Angeles, Chicago, Philadelphia and other cities, we have set for ourselves a triple purpose in the writing of this book.

The first goal to is investigate ways of salvaging out of an intermarriage situation instruments for Jewish survival. Obviously, the conversion of the non-Jewish partner is the optimum; but there are other areas where Judaism can—and must—be kept alive in the intermarried household, especially where children are involved.

The second goal is of equal value: to assuage the pain of the Jewish parents; to erase the frequently-felt feelings of guilt about a son or daughter who has intermarried or is about to do so, and to provide suggestions for dealing with unprecedented family situations which grow out of such a marriage.

Do we approve of intermarriage? It is not a matter of approval or disapproval. We understand that it is sad, sometimes frightening, for a committed Jew to be confronted with an intermarriage situation. As wonderful as the inividuals involved might be, the threat of the identity submersion of the Jewish partner and of his or her children, the total assimilation of the next generation, the evaporation of Jewish values and traditions justifiably scares us.

Cold statistics, however, are made up of warm people; and that brings us to our third purpose in writing the book. We want the partners involved in an intermarriage as well as their families to experience happy, loving, nurturing, honest relationships. In order to do that, they will have to confront a variety of feelings and issues. This book will help them.

The breakthrough concept of the Intermarriage Prenuptial Pact, introduced in the Appendix, will benefit anyone contemplating inter-marriage.

At the same time, we want people to view Judaism as a positive option for defining their religious, spiritual and moral lives.

Above all, we want our fellow Jews to understand that intermarriage is happening, and that we can't preach loyalty to Judaism unless the family, synagogue, rabbi and teacher have made Judaism a viable and exciting element in the life of the Jew.

Perhaps, we, the Jewish community, have been asking the wrong question when we ask "How do we stop intermarriage?" Should the question, rather, not be, "How do we teach people to love Judaism?"

We remind parents caught up in their pain and guilt that their child and his or her love object are also caught up but caught up in their passion and their plans. Your child's lover appears as a stranger to you. How difficult it is to fathom that someone else can now be on more intimate terms with your son or daughter than you. Yet, that is the nature of love, an intense emotional relationship that incorporates romance, physical attraction and deep friendship.

The lovers would just as soon shut out the world as risk losing the attraction, devotion and uniqueness they feel when they are with each other. They have unearthed a treasure, and they want to delight in it!

This book describes practical, day-to-day problem situations and the questions that may arise from them. During the past five years, utilizing our training as journalists, we have had conversations with scores of Jews whose children have intermarried and dozens more who themselves are intermarried. We have spoken also with the children of intermarried couples.

You may read some of the situations set forth on the following pages and say to yourself, "Oh, that could never happen." Be assured: all these situations have been set before us!

Survival, like politics, is "the art of the possible." We Jews had better learn that!

SJJ
BJJ

Appreciation

We would like to thank the many, many people who have shared with us their stories, dilemmas and expectations. We respect their concern for anonymity. We hope our responses help them as well as you, dear reader, to establish a happy and fulfilling family life.

Chapter 1

Why Couldn't He Find a Nice, Jewish Woman? Why Couldn't She Find a Nice, Jewish Man?

My daughter is 29, beautiful, educated with a master's degree, earns a good salary, has many friends, is a gourmet cook who can concoct a walnut dressing for radicchio and arugola, skis without breaking a limb, and she has a sense of humor. Her one-liners are hilarious.

And she's engaged, and he's not Jewish.

How facile it would be to say that we are looking at a generation of yuppies who are wrapped up in charting the stock and bond markets, tasting the zinfandel, plotting their Santa Fe or Eurostyle decor and luxuriating in the thrills of computer software.

But this hardly describes a generation of well-educated, professional, cosmopolitan, young adults who are searching for love, companionship, security and identity in a lonely, often-alienating society.

Most want what most people have always wanted: a home that is a sanctuary from the world, a personal haven.

The media wordsmiths have coined a new word for the home-centered life now being favored by so many people who have dined at all the trendy restaurants, danced at the clubs, taken in all the movies worth viewing and trekked to Paris and Martinique.

The word is "cocooning." Folks are searching for safe harbors from the noise, the crowds, the crime, the pressure, the stress, the perceived harshness of the world, and they have found them right at home.

This is the place where you can be yourself, express yourself and control your own environment. You can watch movies on the VCR, flip through mail order catalogues to order clothes, seeds, books and furniture, paint your walls orange or brown or white or mauve, tend to your plants, play with your dog and cat, lift your weights, sprout your mung beans, write in your journal.

If, in that personal haven, that private space, there is another human being who thinks you're the most special person in the world, one who supports you as you buck the world, what a blessing!

If you were brought up to believe that you should marry a person who is Jewish, you might seriously have looked for one. Then you discover that Jews of the opposite sex to whom you are attracted are not easy to find. In some communities, Jewish women outnumber Jewish men two to one.

Still you search. Once you've graduated from college, you find that the search can be an agonizing and painful one. What may be perceived as a whirlwind round of nights on the town, weekend boat rides and picnics, furtive glances exchanged in the glow of candlelight over intimate suppers are, instead, too often a series of dull dates with people you find boring.

For those who really try hard, it means the ritual of getting dressed up, hair perfectly coiffed, makeup flawless, and driving to a Jewish Singles affair where fine men and women feel as if they are on the market block to be looked over, accepted or rejected on the whim of the moment.

Then, maybe, one day it happens. It could be on a date or at a business lunch or professional conference or jogging or skiing or hiking or at a rally to help the homeless or at an animal rights demonstration.

You start talking with someone, and you realize you never laughed so much. You never enjoyed a conversation so much. You never met anyone so sensitive. You never touched anyone in the same way. You never thought you could share so much with another person.

You are now part of a team, and you feel happy, glowing and darn lucky.

And the person who is making you feel that way isn't Jewish.

The "you" we have been describing might well have been your daughter.

Our son was home for a visit, and we were having dinner at a glitzy Italian bistro. Buddy teaches sociology at a community college 500 miles from our home. He's 34 and never been married. He is one terrific guy. He's the type of person who walks into a room and lights it up with his smile.

When my parents were elderly and found it difficult to get around, it was Buddy who would drive them on shopping excursions and to the park on weekends and make them laugh. He would entertain them with rollicking stories, challenge them to checker matches, assist them with their patio garden and generally seem to help them strip away the fetters of old age.

The product of a good Jewish home and an in-depth Jewish education, Bud even considered becoming a rabbi at one time; or does every Jewish boy think about that right after Bar Mitzvah and Confirmation?

Since he's been teaching at the college—it's five years now—he's attended the synagogue in that town once in a while for services and has taken several Jewish adult education courses.

You have to understand, Buddy loves to teach. He enjoys his students, and, in good humor, has turned aside inquiries from our relatives why he hasn't switched, while he is still young, to a more lucrative career.

The announcement came after the salad vinaigrette, as my husband and I were about to twirl the first forkfuls of pasta primavera. He has met someone, someone unlike anyone he had ever known. He described what she meant to him, all they had in common, the things they both wanted out of life. Then he asked a rhetorical question: Would you dismiss a quality person just because she's not Jewish?

I did the rational, intelligent thing. I burst out crying. My husband lost his appetite.

This will be the first intermarriage in our family on both my husband's side and my side. How should we have answered Buddy?

Your Buddy sounds like a quite a man, someone about whom you have a right to be very proud. From all you've said about him, he must have fallen in love with quite a woman.

To Buddy's rhetorical question, "Would you dismiss a quality person just because she's not Jewish?" the answer has to be a qualifed "Probably not." Unlike the past, in today's world it would be unrealistic to insist, "Yes, get rid of her!"

From your description, Buddy seem to be a talented, non-neurotic, young man who has been raised in a positive and loving environment. We would guess that the light of his eye is of a similar temperament. They should make a terrific couple and terrific parents, optimally within the Jewish community. Would she consider conversion to Judaism?

If, for some reason, she doesn't wish to convert, don't give up on Buddy. He can still remain a committed and contributing member of the Jewish group.

How can our daughter do this to us?

To answer a question with a question, which is a Jewish failing, why do you feel that your daughter is doing something to you? Have you had a difficult relationship in the past? Sometimes, people do profess to fall in love with someone in order to punish another romantic interest or a parent with whom there has been a poor relationship. Of course, the person hurt in the end is himself or herself.

If you honestly feel that you and your daughter have had a rough time and that she is looking to even the score, you are going to have to grapple with your role in the situation.

Have you recognized her for herself or only doled out love based on her accomplishments? Have you respected her opinions or been angry when her views didn't agree with yours?

Have you been too busy with your own affairs to listen to her? Have you hurled insults at each other? Has either of you tried to get revenge before?

If this sounds like a dossier of your relationship with each other, there's some repair work that needs to be done. If you can recognize some of the fault as yours, admit it. There's nothing that eases tension so much as one person saying to another, "I was wrong. I'm sorry! I'd like to discuss this with you."

If things have gone too far, ask your rabbi or another professional to help all of you sort out your feelings.

If your relationship with your daughter has been a good one, an open one, it is doubtful that she chose to hurt you. She probably wants to spare your feelings, but she has fallen in love. When that magical thing happens, the most important person in the world is the love object. It is in this relationship that the highest degree of emotional intimacy is shared.

**Aren't we all being too understanding? If the Jewish commu-
nity were to stand firmly opposed to intermarriage, wouldn't
it be less of a problem? It seems that all the books, workshops
and "outreach" having to deal with intermarriage are almost
rewarding those Jews who have turned their back on their
people.**

The Jewish community is firmly against intermarriage. What has
happened in very recent years, however, is a less rigid and less
judgmental approach toward people who have intermarried. Taking
an unbending position will not stem the tide of intermarriage between Jews and people who aren't which has swept the United States
in the past two decades. There is a respectable consensus that dealing
with each situation on its merits may save many families for
Judaism.

Granted that the Jewish community has to walk a tightrope in
this instance, we must try at one and the same time to discourage
intermarriage where there is room for our influence to be effective
while holding open our options for dealing with a *fait accompli.*

**For a number of years, my son has been saying that Jewish
women are "princesses," that they are materialistic and
spoiled. He has gone out of his way to seek out women who
aren't Jewish. Now he is engaged to a WASP. To my way of
thinking, his fiance can be described as peevish, pampered
and pretentious.**

**At first, I thought Trish, whose coiffure and manicure are
always salon-perfect, was kidding while she explained the
importance of dining out at least once a week at a restaurant
that specializes in five-course *nouvelle cuisine* with a three-fi-
gure tariff. I chortled, but she never cracked a smile; she was
serious. This is a woman who spouts a litany of designers
whose products will not do, while she offers a shorter list of
those she finds acceptable. The glassware must be Baccarat,
the china Rosenthal, the linen hand-embroidered from
France, thank you.**

**My son is successful in his profession, but he can ill-afford
the exclusive neighborhood Trish has selected for their first
residence. When I pointed out to my son the contradictions
of his situation, he rallied with, "Trish is a person with culti-
vated taste and sound financial judgment."**

Stereotyping of Jews as being one thing or another—all wealthy, all conniving, all hook-nosed, all Jewish Princesses—is not limited to non-Jews in general or anti-Semites in specific.

Some members in every minority group have a proclivity for what we know as self-hate, a tearing down of the religious, racial or cultural group into which they are born and, by inference, a rejection of themselves.

This is especially true if the minority group has been disparaged and degraded over the years by the majority group. It's the old story all over again of Hitler's theory that if you repeat a lie often enough it will eventually take on the aspect of truth, no matter how-out-of-sight it is.

Your son is right; there are Jewish Princesses. But there also are Protestant and Catholic Princesses, Italian and Polish Princesses, Princesses of every religion, every nationality, from every continent. Well, maybe there are none from Antarctica.

There are lots of Princes, too a huge number of dandy lads whose haughtiness and self-indulgence ranks them as royal pains.

The royal designation for proper young ladies and gentlemen of the upper middle classes is not confined to any one ethnic or faith group. Any marriage contracted by either party to "escape" from being tied to a stereotype is going to get off to a very false start.

You probably think you've heard them all. Try this one! I am a feminist who has fought for abortion rights and equal pay for women. My husband is an attorney who is a stickler for human rights. We have had a very close relationship with both of our children, Stephen and Bonnie.

Stephen has now brought home the woman of his dreams— and my nightmares. She is a practicing Catholic who is staunchly opposed to abortion and birth control. Stephen says he disagrees with her on these issues, but he loves her.

I am totally uncomfortable with Sally. I've tried to get to know her on other levels, but having to pussyfoot around creates tension. I simply don't want to be in the same room with someone who objects to everything I have believed in and fought for.

The information about Sally's being Catholic is not terribly germane to your dilemma. Try your ideas on abortion and birth control on an equally committed Orthodox Jewish woman, and you may find that the tension is there, also. There are many women in this country who come from the religious right-wing of Judaism and who take a firm stance against many of the criteria of the feminist movement. In the ritual sphere, they are opposed to women being counted in a *minyan,* the quorum necessary to hold a Jewish worship service, or being called to the pulpit for *Torah* honors.

If Stephen has had the close relationship with you and your husband that you report, he must have been exposed to the liberal and possibly radical positions his parents maintain on many issues. Unless his attraction to Sally is a rebellion against the environment in which he has been reared, it may very well cool as he finds himself more and more at variance with Sally's conservative opinions.

There is always the possibility that the discrepancy between Stephen's life style and the rigid, Catholic background from which Sally has come may have been the basis of the attraction she has for him. The idea that "opposites attract"—exogamy, to give it its formal name—is not without foundation. The exotic, even erotic, attraction based on widely differing religious, racial, cultural or ethnic backgrounds, however, usually cannot nourish a long-term romantic commitment.

We understand how you must feel. You do battle for something. Then your own son brings home the "enemy" with the announcement that she is the love of his life. You must be very angry with Stephen. It would be a good idea to get that anger out before it destroys your relationship with him.

Should Stephen's association with Sally continue, know that you do not have to love, like or even respect Sally. You do not have to go out of your way to see her. However, if you totally avoid her, Stephen may avoid you in turn to protect against feeling pulled in two directions.

Here's a suggestion: Don't pussyfoot around. Tell Sally exactly where you stand on the issues of abortion and birth control. And expect that she will enunciate her position. Your views may clash, but Sally might reveal a part of herself that you can endure or even like. It's up to you to determine where Sally will fit in your life.

Let's ponder your options. Can you see her occasionally and be courteous? Do you have to gird yourself to see her to the point where there can be no enjoyment at all in the meeting? Is Stephen willing to see you without her? Consider these options. The choice is yours to make.

Roberta says that Bill, her Protestant fiance, knows more about Judaism than she does. "He's as Jewish as I am," she proclaims.

What has Bill's alleged expertise in things Jewish to do with the realities of this situation? We know an anthropologist who has devoted the better part of her scholarly career to studying the Australian aborigines. She knows their habits, mores and customs. Does that make her an aborigine?

There is a story, probably apocryphal, told about the late playwright, Moss Hart. When he began to make big money, Hart bought a yacht and invited his elderly mother aboard. Dressed in his sailing costume, Moss pointed to the gold braid on his cap and said, "Look, Mama, I'm a captain!" Without hesitation, his mother came back with, "Moish, you know you're a captain, and I know you're a captain, but do the other captains know you're a captain?"

So, too, with Bill. Information about Jews alone doth not a Jew make.

He actually said it! Oh, he wasn't as blunt as he could have been, but our own son asked us if we had to act "that way" when he brings Monica, who is from an old and moneyed Boston Brahmin family, for dinner. "You know, so Jewish." Did we have to talk about eating at the local kosher-style deli? And did we have to invite Uncle Morris, who is so Jewish, at the same time when Monica is visiting the house?

Your son unfortunately, seems to have succumbed to the Self-Hate Syndrome. This condition is not peculiar to Jews; it is to be found among some members of every minority group.

You ought to have a heart-to-heart discussion with your son to find out from whence his Jewish anti-Semitism springs. Has Monica dropped some hints that she is uncomfortable about the too–Jewish environment into which your son introduces her when he brings her to your home? Or is this expression of self-rejection your lad's own creation?

It's about time your son learned the facts of life. Dorothy Parker is credited with having once said that "a kike is a Jew who has left the room." How long does your son intend to camouflage the Jewish home into which he was born, for fear that the Monicas of the world may discover who he is?

We were watching a video last evening. During the action-packed spy thriller, the hero skied down a slalom in Berchtesgaden in the German Alps. Brittany, our eldest son's Lutheran fiancee, said it would be terrific to take a trip to Germany some time. After a few seconds of undecided silence, our other son blurted out that no self-respecting Jew would visit Germany because of the Holocaust. "Wasn't that a long time ago?" Brittany asked. How could she be so insensitive?

Probably, because she isn't aware of what the Holocaust was, what it means to Jews and its impact on Jewish history.

Share your feelings with Brittany. Tell her exactly what images flash in your mind when the Holocaust is mentioned. Explain to her that Berchtesgaden in Southeast Bavaria is where Adolf Hitler's chalet was located. Suggest that she read about the Holocaust or view the many films and videos which are now available on the subject.

Remember, also, that there are Jews who know little or nothing about the Holocaust and who also would say that it happened so long ago that we should stop making a fuss about it.

Of the Four Sons mentioned in the *Haggadah,* the Passover narration, one queried, "What's all this got to do with me?" and another didn't even know enough to inquire. To them and to those like them, we are obligated to tell the story of the Holocaust.

I've told my son, Ivan, that Cynthia will get angry one day and call him a "dirty Jew."

There are men and women of all faiths, races, sizes and shapes, of all nationalities, political persuasions, of diverse educational backgrounds who, when they become angry at others, strike out at vulnerabilities instead of dealing with the issues.

Such persons might call another a "balding idiot," "tight-fisted cad," "elitist snob," and much worse.

Learning to fight fair and to articulate, even rant a bit, about the issues instead of attacking each other is part of the creative communication process in a marriage.

We've all heard stories, especially from older people, about the uncle who marries a non-Jew, only to be called a "dirty Jew" 10 years later and finally comes to his senses.

If Cynthia is a sensitive and kind person, there is no greater chance that she will lash out at Ivan any more than a Jewish woman would denigrate him in some manner.

It is also difficult to use this argument in the face of many viable marriages between Jews and people who aren't and after witnessing the caring and friendship by spouses from both backgrounds during illness or other family crises.

If Ivan and Cynthia remain best friends during their marriage, neither will hurt the other. If they, like so many others, marry for reasons other than deep love and friendship, there will be no end of the demeaning names they may call one another.

Chapter 2

How Can We Stop It?

I told my son that if he doesn't break his engagement to that Gentile woman, I am going to kill myself!

The vocabularies of all ethnic groups contain a similar glossary of threats and imprecations which are made for emphasis: "May I never live to cross the street, if . . . ! "May God strike me dead this very moment, if . . . !"

If you really have suicidal tendencies, we urge you strongly to seek professional help. There are suicide hotlines in many communities.

However, if this is an all-out, last-ditch effort to get your point of view across, we must caution you that it is cruel manipulation. An attempt to control your son through threats of self-inflicted injury on your person could push him away from you.

What is he really trying to do? He is attempting to live his life. You may not like it. No one says you have to. But, if you care about your son and want him to remain in your life, you will immediately replace the threats with some smiles and lots of understanding.

I know I'm supposed to be rational, but ever since Marty told us that he plans to marry Christine I've been sick, physically ill. I sleep fitfully. I have no appetite. I've lost eight pounds.

We understand your feelings. You are angry and out of control, because your son plans to marry someone who isn't Jewish. Your symptoms are similar to those of a mourner, but the grief in your case is directed at a lost dream.

Without attacking Marty or Christine, share your feelings with them. Share the good feelings, also, if you have some. Do you like Christine? If so, tell her. If you don't like her, that's O.K.; you don't have to.

Don't spend all of your time together in serious conversation. Try to relax in each other's company. How about a walk, a movie, a shopping excursion, museum trip? Is it possible that you and Christine share some common interest: plants, cooking, literature, dogs, tennis, computers, a TV series?

Once you've shared your feelings, your mind, released of its load, will be able to send relaxation signals to your body.

Take steps to insure your health. Exercise! Stick to a low fat, low sugar diet!

We're furious that Jeremy plans to marry a girl who isn't Jewish! Shouldn't we just forbid the marriage? He'll forget and find someone else some day.

How old is Jeremy? Unless he's a minor, you can't stop his marriage. If you try, you will just push the two lovers closer, the two of them huddled against the world. Remember the bard and his Romeo and Juliet? If forced to choose, your son may reject you.

Remember, objection rarely works. No one wants to hear "I told you so" or to give in to any kind of pressure.

You say that he'll forget and find someone else some day. What if he doesn't? He might never forgive you for destroying his chance for happiness.

Adults must make their own decisions and take responsibility for their own actions.

What do you think of parents who stipulate in their will that a child will be disinherited if he or she intermarries?

Some people use a will to try and control their children not only during the parents' lifetime but after their death.

"I'm going to cut you out of my will if you do this, that and the other thing." What values are being communicated here? That everything has a dollar tag attached to it?

In demanding that a child marry a Jew, is the parent trying to sabotage an existing relationship with a person who isn't Jewish? Will there also be a stipulation that in the event the child does marry a Jew but happens to fall in love with someone who isn't Jewish, a liaison may be carried on the side? Literature is chock-full of analogous tales.

Such a stipulation can be counter-productive. In the instance of an independent, strong-willed, young person, it can mean an exit visa out of the life of the parents long before their demise.

If money is the control factor in the parents' lives, it is serious evidence of their failure as successful parents and communicators.

This surely isn't the way to teach a love of and appreciation for Judaism and its values.

We told our son that if he marries his non-Jewish girl friend, we will have absolutely nothing to do with him. We haven't heard from him in two months now. How can a son behave like this toward his parents?

Hold on a minute! You told him you wouldn't see him again, right? He took you seriously. Isn't that what you wanted? Parents who make far-out threats or promises to manipulate their children to do their will in any way must be prepared to bear the results, if their bluff is called.

Can't you deprogram a child who is planning an intermarriage, as you deprogram someone who has joined a cult?

Not really, and your assumption that "deprogramming" a cult member is a kind of routine process which is always successful is a very doubtful one. Further, the concept implies that the person who requires deprogramming is in need of a kind of therapy because of his or her abnormal actions which led to membership in the cult. The contemplation of intermarriage cannot be reduced to that simplistic level.

I would prefer that he never marry rather than marry someone who isn't Jewish.

Would you, really? Just stop and think about it. Would you condemn your son to a life of loneliness, a solitary existence bereft of a permanent relationship and children and grandchildren?

No one has a right to play God over the destiny of another, even with the intention of doing the will of God. "The Lord God said, 'It is not good for man to be alone.' . . . Hence a man leaves his father and mother and clings to his wife, so that they become one flesh." *(Genesis 2:18, 24)*

Aren't you getting your priorities confused and allowing yourself to build your prejudices into principles? Your son would not automatically be deserting the Jewish ranks if he married a non-Jewish woman. Granted that it would create many more problems than would marriage to a Jewish woman, there still remain the possibilities discussed a number of times in this book: conversion to Judaism by the non-Jewish spouse, the raising of children in the Jewish faith.

Always, in the background, is the specter of the alternative you are presently suggesting: a solitary existence for your son for the rest of his life.

Why couldn't our rabbi talk our daughter out of a marriage to someone who isn't Jewish?

It often comes as a surprise to some people when we remind them that a rabbi is only human. The rabbi can only use the persuasive powers which he or she has. Nothing supernatural!

If you think that only their parents feel threatened when a man or woman contemplates intermarriage, we can assure you that rabbis feel threatened as well when they see the future survival of the Jewish people becoming wittled down and atrophied.

A rabbi can counsel about the pitfalls in intermarriage, but he or she is trying to buck an intense, passionate, emotional relationship—an almost impossible task.

Do rabbis prefer that Jews remain single rather than marry persons who aren't Jewish?

Your question is painfully blunt, because when one comes to apply theory to real-life situations theory often has to yield. Neither a rabbi, a parent, a friend nor anyone else has the moral right to intervene in the life of another adult except to prevent a criminal act from taking place against another or against one's self.

Obviously, rabbis are concerned about Jewish survival. Like all other committed Jews, they have deep feelings about actions which do or may diminish Jewish identity. As for your specific question, it would be more precise to say that at the point at which a Jewish individual has made a choice to marry out of the Jewish faith, a rabbi ceases to have a further professional interest or to pass judgment.

That may sound callous, but it is the only way for a rabbi to maintain his or her equilibrium in a rapidly-changing society.

Some rabbis would prefer an unmarried Jewish person to one who has married a person who is not Jewish. However, effective rabbis spend less time pointing out the evils of intermarriage and more time teaching Jews to love Judaism.

When did the practice end of sitting *shivah* for a child who had intermarried?

"Sitting *shivah*," observing the Jewish rites of mourning, was not observed for a child who had intermarried. That drastic step was taken in some circles for a child who had become an apostate and converted to Christianity.

Since civil marriage was not the practice in the European community in past centuries, a Jewish son or daughter who married a Gentile was presumed to have been formally converted to Christianity, so that a Christian religious wedding ceremony could be held.

The child who had deserted the Jewish ranks was regarded as having died, mourning rites were observed in the home, and the child's name was never again mentioned in the family circle.

The practice became less and less prevalent as Jews entered the mainstream of social and economic life since the late 19th century.

Could we have avoided our son's intermarriage if we had raised him in an Orthodox home instead of a Reform one?

There are intermarriages in Orthodox families, too. Because of the insulated life-style among ultra-Orthodox Jews, there is little interaction with people who aren't Jewish, so the intermarriage rate probably isn't as high as it is among Jews who interact more with the society around them.

If you would have happiest as Orthodox Jews, then that would have been the right choice for you, but to adopt the trappings of Orthodoxy without the commitment would have frustrated you and appeared phony to your children.

Being Orthodox isn't being more Jewish than being Reform, Conservative or Reconstructionist. It is simply a different way of expressing Judaism. A Jew who places less importance on ritual but studies and thoroughly internalizes the words of the Hebrew prophets and applies them to works of social justice may also be reckoned as a truly religous Jew.

Judaism is a flexible religion that adapts to individual needs, whether they be for prayer and meditation, introspection, ceremonies to mark the cycle of the year and the rites of passage in our lives, concern for social justice, for identification with a people and culture, a tie to history, or a combination of any or all of these.

Those who love Judaism the most are those who are happiest in their Judaism, people who know and understand what Judaism has to offer and make choices accordingly, not those who are captive to denominational labels.

Our Ethan is a medical doctor. And has he had women after him! Not only is he brilliant, but he's handsome, like an Adonis. And he's good-natured, too much for his own good. Well, the female doctors and nurses have noticed all this. They invited him over for breakfast, lunch, dinner and probably for extra-curricular refreshments, too.

In college, he went out only with Jewish girls. Now, he's been lured by these aggressive, non-Jewish females.

Finally, one of these women, a resident in pediatrics, landed this magnificent catch. What can we do?

Is it conceivable that a man as intelligent as your Ethan allowed himself to be caught in a web spun by a wanton woman medic? If your son was being treated to such an enticing round of meals and entertainment, it must have taken a special someone to earn his affections and commitment.

Sometimes, it is so difficult to confront the reality of intermarriage that it becomes tempting to rationalize that your child has somehow been seduced by the non-Jewish person.

Don't women who aren't Jewish look for Jewish men, because they make the best husbands?

There are lots of myths about Jews, most of them negative, which have been handed down among non-Jews. Among the few flattering stereotypes is that of the prototypical Jewish husband.

Maybe there was some truth to the concept in an earlier period in history. For example, there were fewer drunks among Jewish men, squandering their pay checks in the licensed saloon and coming home to beat up on the good wife, who had been slaving over a hot stove all day.

Sociologists have a fancy word, "acculturation," for an old Yiddish saying, *vee es chriselt zich, azoi yiddelt zich."* Freely translated, it means that Jews tend to act in the same manner as do the non-Jews whom they imitate. In other words, "When in Rome . . . "

There is a price Jews have had to pay for their integration into and acceptance by American society. The rate of alcoholism among Jews, once low enough to be a statistical oddity, has increased. Wife abuse among Jews is uncomfortably prevalent, the State of Israel included. The statistics about infidelity among Jewish men and women need take no back seat to the comparable figures among non-Jews.

The non-Jewish female who is set on "catching" a Jewish mate may find that Jewish doesn't guarantee an ideal spouse.

Our daughter says we are hypocrites for objecting to her engagement to a Protestant. She charges that we taught her to respect all peoples and treat all persons as equals. We meant all of these things, but now we question our philosophy. Are we really hypocrites?

Respect for all persons and the belief in the equality of all doesn't have to carry with it a commitment to marry others just to make a point.

It is important to have regard for the integrity of one's own group identity, particularly when that group is a minority constantly confronted by the threat of extinction through absorption within the majority.

You and your husband are not hypocrites just because you do not favor euthanasia for the Jewish group.

Allison is a senior in college. She has had a Bat Mitzvah and was Confirmed. She is getting very serious about Dennis, whom she met at a fraternity party. Dennis is also a senior but not Jewish. An engagement seems imminent.

My wife and I have tried to discuss our feelings about this situation without alienating Allison. She protests that Dennis comes from a family which scorns religion.

"I suppose," she says sarcastically, "it would be all right if I married Brian, Scott or Randy." These young men in her circle of friends are Jewish by birth but have no Jewish commitment. Brian and Scott come from homes which are decked out each Christmas with glittering displays of trees, wreaths, stockings, holly and mistletoe.

Allison wants to know what the difference would be if she married one of her "so-called Jewish" boys instead of Dennis. How do we answer her?

The answer really boils down to how much interest Allison has in her own Jewish identity; how much she would want the home she will establish to be Jewish; how much she wants the children she will bear to consider themselves to be Jewish and to receive a Jewish upbringing.

Her responses to these possibilities are crucial. Illogical as it may appear on the surface, experience has proved time and again that persons who are Jewish only by accident of birth and who grew up in homes lacking Jewish content can still find their way back to the Jewish community, especially when they have children.

We are reminded of a couple who fit this category of apparently having no positive Jewish attitudes when they met and dated. When they decided to marry, it was only to avoid any family friction that they agreed reluctantly to have a rabbi officiate. Their pre-marital conference with the rabbi was a disaster, which they were to relive for their friends later on with a kind of contemptuous amusement. Their Jewish wedding ceremony apparently made no positive impact upon them at all.

When their eldest child was born and came of religious school age, they found themselves "shopping around" for synagogue affiliation in the upper-middle class suburb in which they reside. With their son and, subsequently, his younger sister enrolled in the weekday Hebrew school, the parents found themselves taking an increasing interest in the affairs of the congregation and becoming fond of the rabbi.

The son's Bar Mitzvah was preceded by an entire year by his

MOTHER becoming an adult Bat Mitzvah, she who had never gone to religious school as a child!

Now, the parents are hooked, participating members of their congregation and the local Jewish community.

This could never have happened to Allison's Dennis; he has no Jewish embers to be fired up. Although there can be no guarantee, it might happen to Brian or Scott or Randy.

I don't like the situation at all, but I'm trying to make the best of it. My husband refuses all contact with our son and his non-Jewish wife. He's angry with me for seeing them. He yells that I am disloyal to him and to Judaism. What can I do?

Your husband is entitled to make his own decision. In this case, the decision is to lose his son. He doesn't have the right to ask you to do the same. When he becomes angry with you, quietly but firmly indicate that he has his rights, but that you have yours also. Don't push him.

My girl friend, Bernice, calls me on a daily basis. You can set your clock by this woman. Every weekday morning at 10:30, the phone rings. I don't even say, "Hello," just "Hi, Bernice."

She offers her homespun advice and frequently chatters away about my daughter, Marlene, and Marlene's Protestant fiance, John. "John the Baptist," Bernice calls him.

"Have you told Marlene that he will turn on her?" she asks. "You've got to stop this before it gets any worse," she prattles. "This is what I'd do if Marlene was my daughter," she says. Then she throws in, "My husband's accountant, Stu, is looking for a nice, Jewish girl. Maybe Marlene would like to go out with him?"

Your daughter's personal affairs should not be demeaned by making them fodder for telephone chats. The offer to fix your daughter up is disrespectful and downright rude. Tell Bernice that you can understand her concern, but that you respect Marlene and her decision and don't wish to devote more time to discussing the subject.

Short of telling Bernice to get on her broom and take a ride, don't encourage her by dropping cues that you in any way enjoy or look forward to her daily calls.

My husband, Marvin, is furious with me. He can't understand why I won't join his campaign to break up the engagement of our 24-year-old Reva to Patrick, her Catholic fiance.

"How can you, a former temple sisterhood officer, approve of this action on her part?" he rants.

I can't tell him the reason. It would break his heart. More than 30 years ago, when I was a young woman in my early 20s, I was deeply in love with a young man who wasn't Jewish. For two years, we shared interests, values and our passion for each other.

My parents didn't give me a moment of peace. Even when he offered to convert to Judaism, they threatened, cursed and vowed they would never see me again if I married him. They even dragged the rabbi over to our house, so that he could read me the riot act of what happens to Jews who marry non-Jews.

Both of us were attached to our families and knew that we would be miserable shut off from them. We loved each other desperately but broke up.

Times were so different then. I lost 20 pounds I couldn't afford to lose. "You'll find a nice, Jewish boy, you'll see," my parents assured me. I wouldn't date for a year, and then I dated every Jewish man who asked me out, desperately searching for a Jewish version of my darling. I never found one.

Several years later, I married Marvin. I never loved him. Our daughter has been the joy of my life. Now, she has found that special love and happiness. I see in her eyes the look I had decades ago. I see in her relationship with Pat the depth of friendship and bonding that a person is lucky to find once in a lifetime.

Reva and Patrick are carefully planning their life together, taking into account their religious differences. They are educated and mature and sensitive. But my husband has a phobia. I don't want to hurt him. How can I explain to him what he is doing to Reva?

The end of a relationship is like a death. It requires a period of mourning, allowing the pain and suffering to take their places in our hearts and minds. Not wanting to hurt your husband, you have consigned your memories of your young love to a part of your mind where you cannot have peace, because you can't bring out those memories once in a while and speak about them.

We understand the pain you must have suffered. Please find someone with whom you can speak about your feelings—a very trusted friend or a professional counselor.

With regard to Reva, tell your husband that, at 24, your daughter is an adult who can—and must—make her own decisions. Be friendly and firm. This is the bottom line.

Chapter 3

Breaking the News

My mother is 90 years old. She is a very observant Jew who was born in Galicia and came to the United States when she was 16. Although she learned to speak, read and write English, she's always clung to the idea that Yiddish is the language in which to conduct family discussions.

How do we break the news to Mama of Robin's engagement to a blonde, blue-eyed atheist who was brought up in the Lutheran Church?

Assuming that Mama is in good health and is aware of what happens generally in the family, she is bound to find out. If Robin has a good relationship with her, her grandmother must know something about her grandchild's social life. Your mother has survived many things in her long lifetime. It's not easy to reach 90 and be protected from life's disappointments.

If Robin is close to her, let the news come from her. Her grandmother should know that she is loved and respected. Answer her questions honestly and intelligently, without being condescending or patronizing. Assuming that the wedding ceremony will be a nonsectarian one, let your mother know that her special presence would enrich the event.

Will she be upset, or are you projecting your own feelings, a very natural thing to do?

How do I break the news to my relatives and friends about my son's engagement to a Catholic woman he met in Ireland? My husband's brother and his wife have three children, all of whom have married Jews. As a matter of fact, my brother-and-sister-in-law don't even have any non-Jewish friends. My husband and I have good friends who constantly make derogatory remarks about people who aren't Jewish. Our other friends and relatives aren't much different. Now you can understand the dilemma I have about breaking the news of our son's engagement.

The problem you have is not that of breaking the news; it is the pervasive anti-Gentile atmosphere which seems to permeate your circle of family and friends.

For the sake of your future relations with your son and his wife-to-be, you had better abandon any apologetic approach to family and friends. Your son is marrying someone he loves and whom you, hopefully, will come to treasure, also. And that's that; subject closed; finis!

There is no reward to be anticipated in the world-to-come for anti-Gentile prejudice by Jews. Stereotyping of people who are not Jewish is as evil as stereotyping of Jews by non-Jews. Creating a self-imposed ghetto by associating only with Jews is counter-productive in our open society in the United States. As in any form of self-segregation, it arises from a feeling of inferiority, insecurity and awkwardness in the presence of the majority. It is of no value whatsoever to Jewish survival in this country.

You mention that your son's fiancee is Irish. The Jewish experience in Ireland has been a good one. A former Lord Mayor of Dublin, the late Robert Briscoe, was an observant Jew and a dedicated Zionist. The first Ashkenazi Chief Rabbi of the State of Israel was the late Isaac Herzog, who came to that high post after having served as rabbi in Belfast and Dublin and as Chief Rabbi of the Irish Free State. His son, Chaim Herzog, a native of Ireland, was elected Israel's sixth president in 1983.

Emily was married to a Jewish man who, after three years of their marriage, was womanizing. He wanted everything his way. He abused her verbally and spent every dime the two of them made.

We count our blessings for Jay, the loving, tender, loyal man, the non-Jew to whom she is now married.

But how do I explain this to my friends who wonder why our daughter left a Jewish husband for a non-Jewish one?

Anyone who happened to study logic in college will remember what a false syllogism is. "All men are human. Sally is not a man. Therefore, Sally is not human."

It would be equally illogical to hold that, because Emily was married to a Jew who was unfaithful, all Jewish males are philanderers. It is equally invalid to hold that, because the non-Jewish Jay is loving, tender, loyal, all non-Jewish men share those characteristics.

The problem is not Emily and her new spouse but the cynics in your circle of friends. Tell the buttinskys to butt out!

When we went to visit Brooke at college last fall, she introduced us to Daryl, a smooth, cultured, graduate student in physics. Realizing that something serious was happening between the two, we asked Brooke if Daryl was Jewish. He didn't look Jewish, but his last name could have been a Jewish one. "Of course, he is," Brooke assured her mother and me.

Now, we have the truth. They met at a poetry reading on campus. Daryl asked his friends about Brooke and was told, among other things, that she is Jewish and that she dated only Jewish men. So, he pretended to be Jewish.

They're very serious about each other. Brooke defends him, saying he cared for her so much that he played a role. We say he's deceitful.

We agree with you. Daryl also appears to have a frivolous attitude toward religious and ethnic commitment. However, do not make a major issue of this. Adopt a passive attitude towards the relationship and watch where it goes. We have a visceral feeling that it will fizzle out. If Daryl was deceptive in this situation, chances are that he copes with life's challenges by following a script of deception and pretense.

Maintain a loving nurturing and supportive relationship with Brooke throughout what may prove to be a trying period for her.

Elaine couldn't stop raving about Jeff for the three months before she brought him to the house for dinner. From his looks and last name, we assumed that Jeff was Jewish. Now and then our daughter would allude to Jeff's reactions about

an lsrael-centered news story or his interest in a Bernard Malamud novel that would reinforce our impression.

Now, they're getting married. And, guess who's not Jewish! She knew all along but wanted us to "get to know him without prejudice and like him for himself." Elaine defends her perfidy by saying that she saw no reason to upset us before her plans were definite. We feel deceived.

We understand your feelings about the subterfuge. Was it an out-of-the-ordinary transgression pulled off by two people who are ordinarily sensitive and caring, but who blundered in their endeavor to spare your feelings? Have you done and said things in the past that convinced Elaine that you would be outraged and possibly hysterical at the thought of her marrying a man who is not Jewish? Was Elaine terrified of a showdown?

Whatever the motivation, Elaine and Jeff stumbled over one of their first hurdles in planning their intermarriage. Their prevarication didn't assuage anyone's feelings. Instead, it created more problems. Marriage requires maturity. That means grappling with difficult situations honestly and facing the consequences. If the partners can fool the folks, will they eventually try to fool each other?

Chapter 4

Will the Marriage Work?

We have attended 20 weddings during the past three years. Nine have been between Jews and people who aren't. We are disheartened that more Jews aren't marrying other Jews; but we have to admit we have been gratified to witness warm relationships develop between our friends and their daughters-in-law and sons-in-law who are not Jewish.

These role models made us feel that we could live with the idea if one of our own three children chose to marry a Gentile.

That was before we met Pamela.

Todd, our eldest, brought her home one day in early May. She was blonde, blue-eyed—and an iceberg. All of our attempts at getting her to warm up failed. I commented about the beauty of the jacaronda trees which were displaying their stunning, purple blossoms, and her taciturn response was "Nice."

At first, we attributed her attitude to shyness, but we soon realized that a cast-iron, cultural barrier existed between Pamela and our hugging, teasing, "Are you sure you've had enough soup?" after the second bowl, family.

When we met her parents, they turned out to be stiff, proper, upper-crust, non-ethnic people. They were not at all like the warm Gentiles we had met over the years.

We raised Todd to make his own decisions, and he is 25 years old. Nevertheless, we are stunned and certain that his choice is a mistake.

Do intermarriages work better if they occur between Jews

and people from other ethnic groups rather than with people who are non-ethnic?

It seems to help, especially if the ethnic groups involved are somewhat evenly matched in readiness to display emotions or conceal them, to acknowledge their unique group identities and to treasure their respective ethnic heritages. Some studies, for example, indicate that individuals from an Italian ethnic background with its warm environment get along better with Jews who also come from gregarious families.

However, there is an element of risk here, too. Sometimes, members of an ethnic group who possess all the characteristics we have described may be hostile to members of another ethnic group, in this case to Jews.

Love, companionship, tuning in to each other—wonderful. But aren't there going to be problems in an intermarriage that there wouldn't be in a marriage between two Jewish individuals?

Yes. An intermarriage will require additional communication, compromise and planning, as the couple prepare to grapple with their individual religious identities, relationships with their parents, holiday traditions, the rearing of children, perception of news events and even sensitivity to comments that strike out at religious and cultural vulnerabilities, perhaps even choice of neighborhood and vacation locales.

Won't an intermarriage most likely end in divorce?

When an intermarriage ends in a divorce, it is very convenient to point to the difference in religion as the culprit. Sometimes it is; often, it isn't.

People get divorced because they change. They grow in different directions. They have differing goals. The images of the partners don't flesh out. They panic at the middle-age search for security and roots. They take each other for granted. They stop communicating.

Of course, if you add to this sampling the disparate cultural, ethnic and religious backgrounds in an intermarriage, you place yet another strain on the union.

Under what circumstances does an intermarriage have the least chance for success?

If one partner plays down his or her religious involvement in order to please the other, stress and resentment will build.

How about a couple who say that that their religious differences make absolutely no difference to them, since neither one cares about religion?

This is a facile answer often used to dismiss the nitty-gritty questions which are inevitable in a marriage between persons of different religions.

Even if they have no pronounced feelings now, what will happen when children come? Living in an American society which is very much religion-oriented, at least in lip service, it is not easy to raise children in a religiously sterile environment.

Many young people who take the attitude that apparently is true of the couple you describe find that their feelings change as they get older. By the time they reach middle age, their individual indifference to ties of faith has melted away in a surge of nostalgia for their respective religious roots.

Susan, our daughter, told us that her fiance, Cliff, who is a "non-practicing" Episcopalian, had agreed to raise as Jews the children they someday hope to have. The other night, Susan and Cliff were over to our house for dinner. Toward the end of the meal, while we were munching strawberries and sipping herb tea, the subject of how the children would be raised came up. Cliff denied that he had ever committed himself to raising the kids as Jews. Among other reasons, he pointed out that if they were raised as Jews they might encounter anti-Semitism. Susan was shocked.

Susan and Cliff have a whopper of a problem. Determining how they will raise the children is just a symptom. They are not communicating. If one thinks she heard something, and the other denies that he said it, there is interference on the line.

The only way for them to solve the problem is to recognize that they have one and to seek pre-marital counseling. A communications breakdown can spell trouble for any marriage. In the case of a marriage between persons of different faiths, this is a disaster signal.

If it is possible for them to mend the breakdown, it would be crucial for Cliff to learn about Judaism and anti-Semitism, so he can understand what raising children as Jews really means.

Can't there be serious problems in a marriage between an Orthodox Jew and a Reform Jew?

There sure can! Questions and practices relating to the Jewish dietary laws, prayer, one or two-day New Year and Festival observance, views of the role of the woman, divine revelation and a lot of other matters may cause a strain on the marriage bond.

However, if you infer by the question that a marriage between a Jewish individual and a person of another religious, cultural and ethnic background is no different than the union of an Orthodox Jew and a Reform Jew, then you are way off!

Chapter 5

The Wedding Ceremony

Our son has gone along with his fiancee and agreed to exchange their wedding vows in a church. We don't even want to attend the ceremony. My wife feels it would be an ordeal that she couldn't stomach. I agree.

It is unfair and unrealistic to expect that children will mold their lives to please their parents. It is equally unfair for children to believe that they can embroil their parents in situations which inflict deep psychic and emotional wounds.

If attending the church service will cause your wife and you so much pain, don't attend.

It would be appropriate for you to ask your son if he knows exactly what will happen during the ceremony in church. Will he be called upon to genuflect during the service or to kneel to receive the benediction? Will the blessing of the "Father, the Son and the Holy Spirit" be invoked upon the couple?

Your son should check out the ceremony in advance and not blindly be led to the altar.

What happens during a Christian wedding ceremony?

You mean you don't watch the "soaps" in which there is a full-blown, formal wedding scene ever so often?

What happens depends on what kind of Christian ceremony it is: Roman Catholic, Greek Orthodox, or any one of the many Protestant denominations.

Instead of the parents of the bride and groom escorting them down the aisle, as they would in a Jewish ceremony, the father walks his daughter down and "gives the bride away" to the bridegroom at the altar, while her mother sits in the first row.

The environment is rich with Christian symbols including, again depending on the denomination, crucifix, vestments, candles, chalice and stained glass depictions of the Stations of the Cross.

The ceremony will include references to Jesus and may conclude with the blessing of the newlyweds, "for whom we ask this in the name of Jesus Christ, our Lord."

Some rabbis will officiate at marriages between Jews and people who aren't; others refuse. Why the difference?

Orthodox, Conservative, Reconstructionist and a majority of Reform rabbis will not officiate at a marriage between a person who is Jewish and one who is not.

As teachers and spiritual guides of the Jewish people, rabbis see one of the their principal objectives to be the perpetuation of Judaism. The union of two Jews in marriage implies a future for Judaism in the new home. Between a Jew and a non-Jew, the expectations for Jewish survival are shaky.

The home is an extension of the religious sanctuary. It is the place of Sabbath, festival and holiday celebrations, a locale for learning through Jewish books and music, a place where Jewish identity is enriched.

The Jewish wedding ceremony gives the sanction for a Jewish home. However, many feel that it becomes a charade, a futile choreography, when there is no intention of having a home which will be Jewish.

A number of Reform rabbis will perform intermarriage ceremonies. Some of them require basic study of Judaism, even though they may not require conversion. Others insist on a prior commitment from the couple that the children will be raised as Jews.

These rabbis reason that they don't want to drive the Jewish member of the couple away from Judaism. They also hope that the Gentile might consider converting to Judaism in the future, and they want such a person to have had a previous connection to Judaism and the Jewish community which they see the marriage ceremony as providing.

Does that mean, if I want a rabbi to officiate at my daughter's marriage to her Gentile fiance, there won't be a problem?

It is possible you will find such a rabbi. But, why do you or your daughter and her fiance want the services of a rabbi? Has her fiance examined the nature of a Jewish wedding ceremony, and can he be comfortable with it? How about the feelings of the bridegroom's family?

Has it occurred to you that a judge can perform a civil ceremony in a hotel, garden or home?

But we want the service to be warm and spiritual.

The couple could write their own service and weave poems and other readings into a warm and personalized ceremony.

The vows they exchange might be expressive of how they feel at the moment. Their words, spoken from heart to heart, should warm any ceremony.

The breaking of the glass, the *huppah* marriage canopy, these symbols are so important to me. I can't hold back the tears when I even think about them. When I attend a Jewish wedding, I get weepy. I want these symbols at my child's wedding. Can't we have them at the civil ceremony to be performed by a judge?

These symbols are part of distinctly Jewish experience. The sobering intrusion of shattering glass at the end of the festive nuptials, followed by shouts of *"Mazal Tov!"* from those assembled, belongs to the rich tradition of the Jewish people. So, too, the presence of the bridal pair and their intimate families under the marriage canopy is not a charade but a living testimony to the centuries-old setting in which Jewish men and women have been united in wedlock.

To take these symbols out of context and place them in the setting of a ceremony conducted by a representative of the civil authority smacks of sham and pretense.

If you get teary-eyed at weddings, your eyes will fill up at your child's, also, without the Jewish decor which does not belong in this instance.

Wouldn't it be a great idea, my daughter asks, to have a rabbi and a Christian minister perform her wedding ceremony and include rituals from both religions to symbolize the blending of two faiths?

Even those Reform rabbis who perform marriages between Jews and non-Jews—and they are still considered to be in a minority—will not usually co-officiate with a clergyperson of another religion.

The "blending of two faiths" which your daughter fantasizes is a gossamer dream. You can't just bypass the basic differences, as honest as they are serious, between Judaism and Christianity by staging a make-believe performance at a wedding.

Tell your daughter and her husband-to-be these facts of life. Noble as their intentions are, they should learn that marriage is for real, and reality begins with the wedding ceremony.

We have relatives who are refusing to attend our daughter's wedding, because she is marrying a man who is not Jewish. We attended the weddings of their children. I'm insulted— and furious!

There are many Jews who feel that they are being disloyal to Judaism by attending a wedding ceremony establishing a home which will not be Jewish one. If the ceremony is to be held in church, or if a non-Jewish clergyperson is to officiate, their reaction will be intensified.

These people are facing up to their feelings honestly, even though you may disagree. They may also feel that their presence at the wedding would indicate approval that they would rather not convey to their own children or grandchildren.

It is better to have as wedding guests people who really want to be there. Those who are disgruntled for any reason will not contribute to a happy atmosphere by their presence.

What about all the gifts I gave when their children married?

It would be rude on their part not to send wedding gifts, even if they don't attend the ceremony, especially since you gave wedding gifts to their children. After all, these are your relatives and not just casual acquaintances.

Graham, our future son-in-law, was converted to Judaism two weeks ago. He and Amanda will be married next month. What role can his parents play in the Jewish wedding ceremony? And may the non-Jewish brother and sister of a convert to Judaism hold up the marriage canopy?

Graham's parents can be given exactly the same recognition that you, as Amanda's parents, will be given. That means escorting their son down the aisle, standing at the side of the *huppah* bridal canopy during the ceremony and joining in the recessional following its conclusion.

As for the second part of your query about whether non-Jews are permitted to hold up the portable canopy, they certainly are. The four poles are customarily held up by males, but there is no prohibition against women doing it, nor is there any restriction based on religion.

A person who is not Jewish may serve as best man, maid or matron of honor or ring bearer. He or she is restricted only from serving as one of the two witnesses to the signing of the *ketuvah,* the Jewish marriage contract.

Chapter 6

Will My Grandchildren
Be Jewish?

When our daughter was dating Walter, my husband gave them both a hard time. Sam wouldn't allow Walter in the house and wouldn't even refer to him by name. When the couple, then in their mid-20s, gave themselves a wedding, the father of the bride was noticeable by his non-presence. He had written his daughter off.

Now, they're expecting, and Sam wants to be able to see his first grandchild. What to do?

Sam has come to grips with his own mortality upon hearing that his first grandchild is on the way. The first move will have to be his. No one can mend this relationship for him. He should telephone your daughter and share his positive feelings with her. He obviously shared the negative ones when she married a man who isn't Jewish.

It will take time for the relationshp to be rebuilt, and it can best be accomplished by sharing casual experiences, not stiff, "Let's have dinner together" evenings. Rather, Sam should suggest things he and your daughter enjoyed before. How about walks, apple picking if her pregnant condition permits, a museum trek, movies or planting azaleas?

There is a possibility, of course, that your daughter may reject her father's overtures. She may feel that he is interested only in the child and not in her. Only Sam can convince her otherwise, and time and patience will be needed. Good luck!

My daughter is planning to marry a Gentile. How I can I help their children-to-come, my grandchildren, retain a Jewish identity?

The first thing you will have to do is accept as fact that it will be your daughter and her husband who will raise their children, including making the major decisions about their lives. When and if they will want advice, they will ask for it. And they will love you more and seek you out if you are loving and supportive, not intrusive,

Do not suffocate them with guilt. This is important, because you may end up being the Jewish role model, and a role model who is considered difficult will not have a positive influence.

When the grandchildren come and as they are growing up, don't just tell them how terrific Judaism is. Show them! Provide holiday experiences. Take them to synagogue when appropriate and they are old enough to appreciate children's services.

When they're older, show them how to design a family tree. Use maps and history books to explain what happened to their Jewish family. Begin with their mother, then you. Someday, when they are looking for identity in a world too vast to comprehend, they will recall their roots, their "Jewish connection".

All this, of course, with the knowledge and agreement of your daughter and son-in-law.

Our intermarried son and his wife don't send their children to Jewish school of any kind. Is there anything we as Jewish grandparents can do?

Sure. Ask if they have considered sending the children to Hebrew school or Sunday school. Is money a consideration? If it is, are you in a position to offer help? What about logistics? Do the kids need a ride, or do they have safe bikes that they can ride to synagogue classes?

Or, have your son and daughter-in-law decided not to give their children formal religious education? If so, you'll have to accept their decision.

As with so many situations cited in this book, it is important to express honest emotions but to refrain from pressuring your family. It's their turn to raise children.

How can we influence our grandchildren when we live a continent away?

There's nothing like being together to nurture a relationship, but an active, long-distance relationship can be viewed as an adventure. You can, indeed, reach out and touch. So, write letters, make phone calls. Send thoughtful but not extravagant gifts. Tape and mail videocassettes.

Our son, Nat, married a Catholic woman. They have decided that their first child and our first grandchild, Tiffany Ashley, will be raised Catholic. My husband and I are sick. What makes matters worse, if they possibly can be, is that Nat has asked us not to give Tiffany gifts for Hanukkah or wear jewelry with Hebrew letters in her presence, since it would "confuse" her.

They may rear Tiffany in any way they choose. What they may not do, however, is choose your identity! Who you are and what you are should not be hidden from your granddaughter. She has Jewish grandparents, and that is a reality.

This holds true for the reverse, also. Were your grandchild to be raised a Jew, the grandparents who aren't Jewish shouldn't have to camouflage their religious, cultural or ethnic identities.

A child can be Catholic and have Jewish grandparents. A child can be Jewish and have Catholic grandparents. Or Protestant grandparents, or Buddhist grandparents. All are part of the child's heritage.

Please remember, this child is an independent human being who needs all the love she can get. Make sure Tiffany doesn't become the innocent victim of your disappointment over the fact that she isn't being raised as a Jew.

What if the child is raised without any formal religious training but just learns to be a good person with good, ethical values? How about that as a solution to the dilemma?

It sure sounds like you've hit the jackpot . . . but, hold on! That would mean no Christmas tree or holly or carols, wouldn't it? No Santa Claus. No Easter basket or egg roll.

The world of the secular child or adult is typically a world draped in religious symbols, even though the so-called secularists tend to gloss over that fact.

Would your solution mean that the child would have no exposure and no knowledge of the commitments of the two families that went into the making of the child?

But, aren't there many fine families that practice no religion?

There are many individuals who are non-religious and who lead ethical and moral lives. Oscar Wilde has one of the characters in "The Importance of Being Earnest" observing that being advanced in years "is no guarantee of respectability of character." Neither, we might add, is religious confession or affiliation.

However, you have queried us about fine families and not just individuals. Here, we must hedge somewhat. A family unit, usually including children, has to peg its ethical and moral values on some system, religious or philosophical, which provides guidelines. Having a moral consciousness in the family cannot be left to chance.

What is a non-religious family? Does it ignore Christian religious celebrations such as Christmas or Easter? Does such a family really drop out of the American religious scene, or is there a residue of identification and participation?

That's where the rub comes in, when the children of an intermarriage are involved.

My grandchildren are the product of an intermarriage. Their parents say the children will select their own religion when they mature. They say it's not fair to impose religion on a child.

Religion is such a strong institution that it is virtually impossible to ignore it in a child's development. If the parents fail to expose the child to a religion, others will. Friends, neighbors, teachers, club leaders, all will in one way or another allude to religion at some time as they interact with the child.

Whether we approve, American society places more of an emphasis on religious identity than we may want to admit. Society seems to abhor a vacuum when it comes to religious identity. Early on, the child is asked to stand up and be counted religiously.

To opt for no religion is really to become a secular Christian, an individual who superficially celebrates Christmas and Easter.

Often, when the child has no spiritual identity, he or she is ripe to be seduced by a cult which will tantalize the young person with love, warmth and a sense of spiritual fulfillment, however synthetic it may be.

What if one child of an intermarried couple is raised in one religion, and the other child is raised in another?

Utter chaos, we would imagine. Confusion compounded.

How will parents who have different religions select one faith over another for their children?

There are several possibilities. One of the parents may be more committed to his or her religious faith. One of the parents may play a more passive role in the marriage relationship, turning to the stronger mate in the decision-making process.

Should the former religion of the parent who has been converted to Judaism be concealed from the couple's children?

Definitely not! This is not a skeleton-in-the-closet situation. When the child or children are mature enough to understand, the intellectual process which led the formerly non-Jewish parent to become Jewish should be explained. It will serve, also, to enhance the appreciation of the children for their Jewish heritage.

His parents have decided that our grandson, Richard, will not receive a formal religious upbringing in either Judaism or in the Presbyterian church in which his mother was raised. However, the *machatonim* (in-laws) keep heaping upon Richard books about Jesus and other New Testament stories. In December, their ranch house becomes a child's Christmas come to life. How can we counter this?

Don't we have a contradiction here? Richard's parents have agreed not to give the boy a religious upbringing. How, then can they be passive when your daughter-in-law's parents violate the agreement by plying Richard with books about Christianity?

It would be wrong to prohibit Richard from attending celebrations on either side of the family. These events are part of his grandparents' lives and make for rich, warm memories that will last Richard throughout his life.

It would be equally wrong for Richard or any child to assume that Christmas is anything but a religious holiday. As the gorgeous decorations, carols, special gifts and delicious foods tantalize the senses and transform the bleak, dreary winter solstice into a magical time, it is urgent to recognize the day as the celebration of the birth of Jesus.

A quagmire? It is.

The reality is that in an intermarriage a child is exposed to different religious influences. Richard has Presbyterian grandparents, and he has Jewish grandparents. Both sets of grandparents should be discouraged from vying for Richard's religious loyalties.

There is nothing sadder in an intermarriage and nothing more potentially harmful to the children of such a marriage than grandparents fighting a religious duel over the helpless grandchildren.

My daughter is married to a man who is Jewish, and they have a son who is preparing for his *Bar Mitzvah*. The problem is that my son-in-law has a 15-year-old daughter from his former marriage to a Catholic woman. The daughter has been raised Catholic and always wears a cross.

My son-in-law wants his daughter to be in the family photograph and in the video of the *Bar Mitzvah*. I don't think she should be wearing her cross in either. I think the whole thing is a mockery. This is a Jewish function, and she's not Jewish.

If the young woman wears a cross all the time, it would be tasteless as well as unethical to propose that she appear incognito in the photos and video of her step-brother's *Bar Mitzvah*. Your grandson has a step-sister who is Catholic, and that's a family fact.

The Jewish significance of the event will not depend on whether someone present is seen with her symbol of Christian identity. More important is whether your grandson will carry his own Jewish identity into his adult years by continuing his Jewish commitment beyond the *Bar Mitzvah* date.

I'm angry! My son is married to a wonderful woman who isn't Jewish. She says she can't convert, because of the hurt it would cause her parents. She says they would feel as if she were rejecting them.

When they went to enroll their two children in the Sunday School of a synagogue, the rabbi said that the two children aren't Jewish and would have to convert to Judaism.

The family is being cut off from the Jewish community, and my grandchildren will be lost to Judaism!

You raise one of the stickiest dilemmas in contemporary Jewish life and a source of controversy between Reform and Reconstructionist denominations on the one hand and the Orthodox and Conservative movements on the other.

According to *Halacha,* Rabbinic law, the line of descent is through the mother. The Jewishness of the mother determines the Jewishness of her child or children.

In the early 1980s, the (Reform) Central Conference of American Rabbis adopted the "patrilinear" principle, which recognizes a child as being Jewish if his or her father is Jewish, even if the mother is not.

The Reconstructionist denomination in Judaism also follows this rule.

The Orthodox and Conservative denominations vigorously oppose the concept of patrilinear descent, with the Orthodox even threatening to invalidate marriages between their adherents and Reform or Reconstructionist Jews, because there will be no proof that they are authentic Jews by reason of their heritage.

Unfortunately, your son and his wife and your two grandchildren are victims of this controversy. It would seem that the logical move for them to make would be to seek affiliation with either a Reform or a Reconstructionist congregation. The rabbi who pronounced the children as being non-Jewish was undoubtedly either Orthodox or Conservative.

Our daughter, Anne, is married to Trevor, a loving man who is a practicing Roman Catholic. My other daughter's son will be celebrating his *Bar Mitzvah* in six weeks. Both daughters have decided that Trevor should get a non-speaking *aliyah*, pulpit honor, at the Bar Mitzvah service.

When I indicated that the rabbi might object, because only Jews should receive *aliyot*, they said that what the rabbi didn't know wouldn't hurt him. Anyhow, it's their event.

I feel that the rabbi, who is my rabbi as well as my grandson's, should be told. But if I tell him, my daughter will be furious with me. How should I handle this dilemma?

Before it is too late, have a serious discussion with the parents of the *Bar Mitzvah*. Tell them that if they go ahead with their plans they will be making a charade of the *Bar Mitzvah* service instead of the meaningful spiritual event it should be.

What kind of an impact could this subterfuge possibly have upon their son, the *Bar Mitzvah,* to know that his Uncle Trevor is being co-opted into the *Torah* service under false pretenses, while an unsuspecting rabbi gives unwitting approval?

Furthermore, tell your daughter and son-in-law that you absolutely refuse to be a party to this deception and that you will have no recourse but to go to the rabbi with the truth.

Until recent decades, the problem would have been moot, because Trevor would have been prohibited by his Catholic faith from attending a non-Catholic religious service, let alone participating in it from the pulpit. Much has happened in the flexibility on the part of the church in this area, and the dilemma you pose is symptomatic.

They are expecting our first grandchild and have announced that, if the baby is a boy, he will be named Christopher after our son-in-law's favorite uncle. Could a name be more Christian?

No, with the possible exception of "Jesus" as a given name. Christopher means "bearer of Christ" and comes from the Greek and Latin. We imagine that you have heard of Saint Christopher, the patron saint of travelers.

My son's wife is not Jewish, but their 9-year-old Sharon has been raised as a Jew. Now, the parents are getting divorced, and my-soon-to-be ex-daughter-in-law will be getting custody of the child, whom she says will now be raised Baptist. I'm concerned over the confusion Sharon is bound to experience. What can I do?

You can do absolutely nothing. This is a matter for the court to decide. Hasn't there been any discussion between your son and his wife or between their respective divorce attorneys about Sharon's future religious upbringing? The court must be made aware of your son's feelings and the psychological trauma for a 9-year-old child who is suddenly asked to switch her religious loyalties.

When we refer to your son's feelings, we are assuming that he shares the same ones you have about the situation. If he is indifferent, there is nothing you can or have the right to do as a grandparent.

Divorce is always hard on the kids. It is especially difficult when the parents are from two different religious, cultural or ethnic backgrounds. Your grandchild's case is further evidence. Even if her mother were to be cooperative in the matter of raising Sharon Jewishly, how could she possibly do so in a nominally Baptist household?

My son was married to a woman who had converted to Judaism. They have two children. They were divorced a couple of years ago, and my son subsequently married a woman who had been born Jewish. My former daughter-in-law retained custody of both children, but my son has flexible visiting privileges, which he exercises.

My former daughter-in-law returned to being a Catholic. One of their two children, my grandson, Daniel, recently celebrated his *Bar Mitzvah*. My son made sure that he and his present wife had the regular pulpit honors that go with a *Bar Mitzvah* in their temple. Daniel's mother was upset by this. She didn't have any right to be upset, did she? What is the role of the non-Jewish parent in a *Bar* or *Bat Mitzvah* ceremony?

We find it curious that you make no mention of Daniel's feelings in this situation. Certainly, the 13-year-old must have had some preference. Was there any family conference or discussion about the matter, or did the boy's father act arbitrarily?

It is disturbing to hear of any case where a stepparent thrusts himself or herself into a role which properly belongs to a living parent. If Daniel has enjoyed a very close relationship with his stepmother, and if so desired, she could have been offered a part, but not one in which she displaced his mother.

The non-Jewish parent definitely should have some role in the *Bar* or *Bat Mitzvah* service, if he or she wishes to and if it would make the occasion even more meaningful for the celebrant.

The nature of the participation by the non-Jewish mother or father, however, would have to be different than that by a Jewish parent.

For example, he or she might be given a non-speaking role or, if a speaking part in the service, it would have to be a prayer or blessing adapted to the special occasion. The Central Conference of American Rabbis, the national organization of Reform rabbis, has resources for such special parts.

All this is based on your report that Daniel's Roman Catholic mother wanted to take part in her son's *Bar Mitzvah*. It is unfortunate that her feelings were not taken into account, and the *Bar Mitzvah* boy's feelings, also.

Sanford's non-Jewish wife received custody of their son, Marc, in the recent divorce settlement. Now 10 years old, Marc attended Hebrew school until his father moved out of the house when the divorce proceedings began. Now, Marcy, Marc's mother, refuses to drive the boy to the temple school, which is about four miles from their home. She apparently has no interest in having Marc remain Jewish. What can my son do? What can anyone do?

Since his mother has custody, she will have the greatest influence over Marc's life. She may feel she sent her son to Hebrew school to please his father, who no longer is now a part of her life, or as part of an agreement in effect during their marriage but which has now been abrogated.

If the divorce was an unfriendly one, Marcy may feel that she doesn't want to encourage any activity which will strengthen Marc's identity with his father.

Does Marcy work? Does she have a flexible schedule which would allow her to chauffeur the boy? In the event that she is willing to have Marc attend Hebrew school but can't drive him, can his father? Can you? Can Sanford hire someone to drive Marc? Are there Jewish religious school classes closer to home to which Marc can walk or ride his bike?

Whatever the alternatives, Marc must not be caught up in the crossfire of factions yanking him to identify with one religion or another. Discussions between Marcy and Sanford concerning Marc's Hebrew school studies must be conducted on a factual basis. Marc's father needs to know exactly why his ex-wife won't or can't drive their son, and then be prepared to offer options.

The many problems which confront intermarried couples in selecting religious experiences for their children are far more serious when there is a divorce, and the child's religious identity becomes a part of the adversarial struggle.

My Gentile son-in-law wants to have his first child baptized, just in case the boy wants to be a Christian later. Won't the baptism make my grandson Christian?

All denominations within Judaism subscribe to the opinion that a child born of a Jewish mother—in this instance, your daughter—is Jewish. Christian baptism, especially since it would be taking place in the case of a child rather than a consenting adult, would not alter the situation. Rest assured, your grandson would continue to be accepted as a Jew.

A more serious consideration should be your son-law's attitude toward his child's religious identity. Does this reflect a violation on her husband's part of an agreement he had with your daughter to raise the child or children in Judaism? Had a consensus been arrived at between them before their marriage or before the birth of their first child? Or was this important subject left hanging, with each parent "inferring" what would happen?

The non-Jewish wife's parents bought Ellie, their 7-year-old granddaughter, a cross to wear on a pendant. The child's mother says she should be allowed to wear the solid gold gift, so that her grandparents won't feel rejected. Ellie shouldn't be confused about why she can't use the gift from people whom she loves dearly, her mother says.
Ellie's Jewish father is annoyed and confused.

The cross isn't an ordinary piece of jewelry. Neither is a six-pointed Star of David. Each is a symbol of religious identification which calls attention to the wearer's pride in and commitment to her or his religious faith. These symbols are not to be worn as casual ornaments.

Wearing a cross could cause a considerable amount of confusion for a child who is identifying as a Jew. Children are as inquisitive as they are blunt. Her school chums might badger Ellie with questions which a 7-year-old might find very difficult to answer. Does her mother think Ellie is equipped to field queries such as "I thought you are Jewish. When did you turn Christian?"

We hope that Ellie's other grandparents feel sufficiently a part of her life, so they have no need to adorn her with a symbol of their faith.

My son and his wife, who was raised Catholic, are sending Alan to Catholic parochial school. They maintain this has nothing to do with religion, and that the decision was made because of all the drugs available at the local public school and the tough kids who hang out there. They also say that the Catholic school has higher academic standards. They checked into other private schools but could not handle the tuition costs. I say Alan will become Catholic. What do you think?

The possibility that Alan will become an adherent of the Roman Catholic faith as the result of his childhood exposure to the religious environment of a parochial school is as likely as it is logical.

We know a man, now in his 60s, who told us that when he was a child in Sydney, Australia, his Orthodox Jewish parents enrolled him in the kindergarten of a Catholic school, because it was convenient to their home, and they felt that nothing startling could happen in a kindergarten class.

The first Friday night after the child's enrollment, as his father finished chanting the Sabbath Eve *Kiddush* over the wine, the kindergarten novitiate piped up with a closing, "In the name of the Father, the Son and the Holy Spirit!"

On the following Monday, he was not returned to the Catholic school!

Won't my grandson be exposed to anti-Semitic instruction if he attends a Christian church or school?

If your grandchild is raised in the church, he will quite naturally be exposed to holidays, symbols and a liturgy which are alien to Jews. He will now be a part of the "other," the religious entity feared throughout Jewish history.

For you, as a grandparent, it will take a special effort to stand back and love your grandson for himself. The challenge to you will be to share things with him other than a common religious identity, if you are not to reject him altogether.

Non-Jewish grandparents face the same situation if the grandchild is being raised as a Jew, although, for many historic reasons, it is easier for a Christian to accept Jewish customs and traditions based on what they view as the "old" Testament than it is for Jews to reconcile with the Christian traditions embodied in the "new" Testament.

Will your grandson be exposed to anti-Semitism in the teaching that takes place in a Christian school? Although the situation has improved markedly in recent years, a part of the instruction in Protestant and Catholic schools, including the content of textbooks which the students are given to read, still contains an anti-Jewish bias.

The students may learn a lesson from the Gospels, "the essence of which is to portray the Jews of Jesus' time as hypocrites or villains or bloodthirsty," according to the late Bible scholar, Rabbi Samuel Sandmel.

The nub of the problem is that Christian writings, from the Gospels on, have portrayed Judaism, at best, as a religion which was superseded and improved upon by Christianity and, is therefore, inadequate or only partially valid and, at worst, as "the synagogue of Satan." *(Revelation 2:9, 3:9)*

The books of Matthew and John, chronologically the last of the Gospels, have been characterized as the most hostile to Judaism. You can imagine how they would be interpreted to a class by an unsympathetic teacher in a Christian religious school!

This is the reality that your grandson may face in a Catholic or Protestant religious school.

Chapter 7

Mistletoe and Matzah

Our daughter-in-law refuses to attend our Jewish holiday gatherings. In the three years she and my son have been married, she has rejected each Passover *seder* invitation, kept away from every *Hanukkah* gathering and won't even drop in on the open house we customarily hold on *Rosh Hashanah*. What can we do?

That depends on the relationship you share apart from holiday affairs. If it is a generally strained relationship, obviously nothing can be done to end her boycott of Jewish functions, unless the total situation is improved.

However, if she is generally on good terms with you, keep the invitations to *seder*, *Hanukkah* and other holiday parties, New Year receptions open.

Perhaps your daughter-in-law feels unsure about what to do, how to act, what happens at these Jewish gatherings. Let her know that she's welcome and wanted. Part of this consists of explaining the holidays before they occur. Then she can decide whether she wants to participate.

Should we invite our daughter's non-Jewish husband to High Holy Day services?

Of course. The invitation should be both to your daughter and your son-in-law to join the family at *Rosh Hashanah* and *Yom Kippur* services.

He'll enjoy the services more if your daughter or you would explain beforehand the meaning of the holy days and what he may expect to see and hear at the services.

This year, our daughter married a man who isn't Jewish. She insisted that we attend the first Christmas celebration in their home. When we declined the invitation, she said we're snubbing her husband and her.

Because your daughter chooses to label your decision a snub doesn't make it so. Have you gotten across to her that you would feel uncomfortable, ill-at-ease in attending a Christmas celebration—replete with a tree and all the "trimmings," we imagine—in the home of your child who was raised as a Jew?

We refer specifically to a Christmas gathering held in your daughter's home. If the same celebration were held in the home of your non-Jewish son-in-law's parents, for example, you might feel no problem in accepting an invitation and attending as a courtesy.

Should your daughter counter that she and her husband have accepted invitations from you to attend Jewish holiday gatherings in your home, you may want to point out that she is your daughter taking part, as she has from childhood on, in Jewish observances in her family home.

Our daughter's in-laws told our granddaughter in front of us that it's a good thing that she has one set of Christian grandparents, so she can celebrate Christmas and Easter, because Jews have to miss out on these terrific holidays.

It is deplorable that any child be put in the frustrating position of a pawn between grandparents or parents.

We hope that your granddaughter already knows that Jews have a year filled with wonderful Jewish times: Sabbath dinners replete with tasty foods, table songs and the happy sharing of the week's activities; *Purim* carnivals; *Hanukkah* parties; good Passover *seders* with well-told narration, songs and *afikoman* searches; snacks and meals enjoyed al fresco on Sukkot.

For majesty, pomp and circumstance as she grows into adulthood, your granddaughter will find the pageantry and the music of *Rosh Hashanah,* the Jewish New Year, and *Yom Kippur,* the Day of Atonement. As she grows up, there will be the round of *Bat* and *Bar Mitzvah* services and receptions for her girl friends and boy friends.

So, help your granddaughter experience as many of these thrilling and heart-warming Jewish events as possible.

Meanwhile, take your daughter's in-laws aside. Explain your feelings. While their remark was in the poorest of taste, it is possible that it slipped out in innocence. Have you tried inviting them to any of your Jewish celebrations? Maybe they feel left out in a divided family.

You mean it would be O.K. to invite them?

Of course. It would a warm, bonding thing to do.

What if they invite us to their Christmas party?

Go, and enjoy.

Wouldn't that be disloyal to Judaism?

Not at all. If you were the hosts at a Christmas party, it would be, but not if you share in the festivities at a Christian home.

Before they were married, my son, Adam, and his wife, Jill, who isn't Jewish, agreed that their children would be raised as Jews. Jill wasn't raised with any religious commitment and felt she couldn't convert to Judaism, because she just doesn't like religion.

Joey, our first grandchild, is now 8. His mother is hedging about enrolling him in the local synagogue school. Despite her avowed dislike of religion, she has a Christmas tree and stockings every year. My son gets very angry about this, but Jill protests that Joey should not miss out on the wonderful things she enjoyed when she was a child. "It just wouldn't be fair to him," she says. She also points out that many Jewish children have trees and stockings.

Would you agree with me that Jill should be criticized for reneging on the agreement?

In the early stages of her romantic commitment to Adam, Jill probably wanted, in all good faith, to please him and be accepted by his family. Children were not part of the real scene; they were in the dream world of the future.

Now, Joey is for real, and Jill might be frightened at turning over a part of him to something that is strange to her, something she feels left out of, even if it is by her choice.

She has also recognized another reality; there are Jews who celebrate Christmas. She might well perceive that Joey can just be Jewish, if that will make Adam happy; but he sure doesn't have to do anything about it. After all, how many Jews do?

My Gentile daughter-in-law insists on having an icicle-and-toy-festooned Christmas tree in her and my son's home. How can I graciously tell her that this is wrong?

You can't, because it isn't. She is not Jewish, and it's her home, too.

If children should know about the heritage of both parents, shouldn't they celebrate the holidays of both, holidays such as Christmas and *Hanukkah*?

If this is a household where one of the parents is a convert to Judaism, we answered previously that his or her former religion should not be concealed from the couple's children. That does not mean, however, that the special occasion of the convert's former religion should be observed. The parent who had been a Christian would not observe Christmas in the home shared with his or her Jewish spouse.

When the parents retain their separate religious identities, each has the right to observe his or her religious holidays and customs. In an instance where one parent is Jewish and the other Christian, it is conceivable that the children would be exposed to both *Hanukkah* and Christmas or Passover and Easter in the home at the same time.

What this does to the children's equilibrium, we leave to your imagination. The holiday seasons become a mish-mash, a jumble of often contradictory and, certainly, unrelated historical happenings, particularly in the instance of *Hanukkah* and Christmas, which have nothing whatsoever to do with each other, except that they both occur at the time of the winter solstice.

Religions depend on rituals and symbols to get across their particular and peculiar values and outlooks on life and death. Trying to throw everything into the melting pot can be very confusing for a child.

Our *Hanukkah* gifts to our grandchildren this year showed up under the Christmas tree as presents brought by Santa. We were flabbergasted and told our son so. He said we were over-reacting. Were we?

Not at all. To lose the significance of the *Hanukkah* festival and its glorious message of religious freedom and have it replaced by Jolly St. Nick and Rudolf the Red-Nosed would be shameful. Your son should know that you are not prepared to deny your grandchildren their rightful exposure to the grandeur of Hanukkah, which has all it can do to keep afloat in the sea of Yuletide carols and decor.

My daughter, Marla, is 45. She was married for 15 years to a Jewish man and had two beautiful children with him. They were divorced two years ago. Last year, she met Frank, an Italian Catholic, and they became good friends. The friendship evolved into romance, and they began to spend all their free time together. He's very well-to-do and treated her to lavish vacations, gourmet dinners and the best seats at the opera and ballet. His children by a previous marriage are grown and close to their father, who is a warm, outgoing man.

Frank asked Marla to marry him. He suggested they sell their respective houses and build a glass and wood paradise on a lakeside lot in a fine suburb.

After their marriage, he helped plan her son's *Bar Mitzvah*, but in no way attempted to usurp the role of the boy's father. He really is a decent guy; and, candidly, when your daughter is 45 and has two teen-agers, you don't ask her to hold out for a Jewish man.

Everything was fine until December rolled around. Frank told Marla it was time to plan the annual Christmas bash. The house was to be decorated not just with a tree but with the works, and the parties were to last for several days.

My daughter couldn't believe this was happening in her home; but Frank insisted and won. She feels he had no right to treat her this way. What do you think?

We assume from your description of the evolution of Marla's relationship with Frank, from friendship through courtship to marriage, that this was not an overnight matter. Didn't one Christmas or one Easter come by during the months they knew each other, so Marla would have had an opportunity to see how important these

Christian observances were to her new man?

Did she think that all of his strong feelings and memories would be dispelled or submerged once he had a Jewish wife?

This is another by-product of lack of communication between a man and woman who come from differing religious traditions and who are contemplating setting up house together.

It cannot be expected that the person who isn't Jewish will have to do all the changing and adjusting.

Chapter 8

The In-Laws

We're dreading meeting Liz's mother and father, who have been described to us as fundamentalist Christians. When they first met our Robby, they asked him to which Hebrew tribe he belonged!

You must display "Christian charity" in this meeting! Liz's parents are probably more alarmed at meeting you than you are in dread of the encounter. Considering the query with which they confronted Robby, they could be surprised that his parents do not have horns!

Keep in mind that there are many, many folks who have seldom or never come in contact with Jews, and whose knowledge of Jews arises out of a reading of the "old" Testament from a New Testament bias.

This accounts for the question that was put to Robby about his tribal affiliation. To Liz's parents, and to many others, today's Jews are still the Hebrews of the "old" Testament, living in a kind of suspended animation in history until their eyes are opened and they accept Jesus of Nazareth as the Messiah, crucified and resurrected.

Our son-in-law's parents are Bible-thumping, born-again Christians, and every time we have to see them they drive us up the wall. They want to debate Biblical passages. We don't want to skirmish with them; we just want to relax. What should we do?

Tell them exactly that. "We would enjoy being with you much more, if the get-togethers did not turn into theological jousts."

You might also point out that they are not going to prove anything by quoting from the Bible to prove that the coming of Jesus was predicted in what they consider the "old" Testament.

You may be wasting your breath, but it's worth the effort to tell them that in almost any discussion Biblical verses can be brought forward on either side of a question. In the years before the War Between the States, clergymen on both sides of the slavery issue cited verses from the Bible to prop up their respective positions.

Cotton Mather, a dominant figure among early American preachers, recorded in his diary for July 4-5, 1712, a "Vigil prayer. For the conversion of the poor Jew, who is this Day returned once more unto New England, and who now for 19 years together been the Subject of our Cares and Hopes, and Prayers."

Sixteen years later, Mather passed on, his prayers for the conversion of the "poor Jew" unanswered.

What do you do when you are sitting down at your daughter and son-in-law's home for what you expected would be a lovely Thanksgiving dinner, the first the couple have hosted in their year and a half of marriage, when his father asks all of us to bow our heads while he delivers a blessing and then proceeds to carry on about Jesus the Savior for—yes, I timed it—a full seven minutes, while we listened, eyes shut, holding hands?

My wife and I were not thrilled whn Joy intermarried, but we didn't want to lose our daughter. Larry, her husband, is a likeable-enough guy, we decided, once we allowed ourselves to get to know him. But on this occasion we felt as if we had been kicked in our stomachs.

You should sit down with your daughter and her husband and tell them exactly how you felt. Assuming they share your feelings, Larry should inform his father that theirs is a neutral religious zone, so that this exhibition of poor manners will not occur again in Joy and Larry's home.

Larry's father must be very insensitive to impose his religious phraseology on a captive audience gathered around the festive board in the home of his son and daughter-in-law. Did he think he would earn evangelical Brownie points at his next prayer meeting for trying to open the eyes of the benighted, heathen in-laws?

Or is he one of those religious imperialists who think that the entire world, Eastern as well as Western, Jew, Muslim, Hindu, Buddhist, Shintoist, all fall under the rubric of the Trinity?

One day last summer, when we were visiting our daughter, Barb, and her husband, Roger, a non-practicing Protestant, Barb took me, her sister-in-law, Kim, and Kim's two children to a theme amusement park two hours away from the suburb where they all live. My husband and Roger went to play golf.

After we'd been driving for about an hour, the children started to squirm. They became bored with calling out the license plates of 17 states and matching wits in alphabet games. So Kim pulled out of her travel bag a book of New Testament stories for children. She and the kids swapped turns reading about the Nativity, the Crucifixion and the Resurrection and how the Jews were responsible for the death of Jesus.

I almost choked on the apple I was chomping. When I caught my breath, I blurted out that I didn't think anyone was teaching that nonsense any more. "That story isn't true!" I insisted. Kim said I was overreacting. They were only children. Besides, this was part of their scriptural reading.

I continued to maintain that it was wrong. Kim then threw out a painful salvo. "It's up to our minister to tell us what's right and what's wrong about scripture and church history. And if you're implying that I'm anti-Semitic, forget it; I'm not. Now, let's relax and enjoy the day."

Barb remained quiet. But, later, while we were wandering around the park, she expressed regret that I had intervened. It would just cause trouble in the family. Roger didn't believe in religion at all, but his sister was a strict Fundamentalist with beliefs sunk in cement.

Was I wrong to mix in?

Absolutely not. Silence implies agreement. The Jews did not kill Jesus. To perpetuate that myth in any way is to fertilize anti-Semitism. Kim's children are getting heavy doses of the fertilizer. Peace in the family cannot be maintained by shoving this very serious problem under wraps. It must be brought out in the open where it can be tackled. Kim may never change her religious perspective or the nature of her children's religious education, but the correct information should be given to her by Barb and Roger. Roger's implied neutrality connotes agreement with Kim's point of view. The "it's no big deal" attitude can be lethal.

I am very sensitive to anti-Semitism. I know that if my son brings home an apparently fine woman who isn't Jewish, lurking in the background may be an anti-Semitic parent, brother, aunt or grandmother. How can I make my son realize this ahead of time, so that he will be sure to marry a Jewish woman?

Most Jews are traumatized every time groups of neo-Nazis or Ku Kluxers march, or when a synagogue is vandalized or a self-proclaimed truth-bearer hawks myths about Jews running the country and absorbing all the wealth.

We quiver when Israel, the ultimate safety net, is threatened or does something to call attention to the imperfections of its people or their leaders.

We are fearful when the evening grows late, and the small talk turns to speculation about whether "it could happen here," and when we hear the accounts or have our own experiences of resorts and country clubs that remain *Judenrein,* "free of Jews."

There is the lingering horror of the Holocaust. We remember that German Jews were intermarried in great numbers, and still they couldn't hide or escape.

We look at our close friends who aren't Jewish and wonder what they would have done in Nazi Germany.

All of this comes to mind, and you make an emotional tie-up with the non-Jewish person confronting you, the individual your son or daughter introduces as his or her beloved. Your stomach turns somersaults, and you are scared.

It is then that we must do the most Jewish thing we can. We must evaluate the person as an individual, just the way we want to be judged. Above all, don't make this man or woman who has been brought into your home the scapegoat for centuries of persecution of Jews.

What happens when the other side of the family has anti-Semites?

Presumably, there will be little social contact between you of mutual choosing. In the unlikely event of your being brought together, the best that can be expected is a cool, hands-off relationship in the expectation of avoiding a hostile confrontation.

Failing these preventative measures, you should simply refuse to be placed in an uncomfortable environment. There are limits to what a person must do preserve peace in the family.

Aren't all non-Jewish people just a little anti-Semitic?

Jews, like all members of minority groups, have traditionally accustomed themselves to keeping a watchful eye out for hints of prejudice when they come in social or business contact with members of the majority.

This is plain, old-fashioned common sense, but it can easily grow into paranoia, as in the story of the two psychiatrists who entered an elevator on the ground floor of the building in which they had their respective offices.

"Have a good day," said one jovially as he exited at his floor, leaving the other psychiatrist to speculate darkly, "What did he really mean?"

Anti-Semitic parents do not necessarily produce anti-Semitic children, although the likelihood of transmission is certainly there. Anti-Semitism arises from a variety of causes: social, economic, cultural, religious, ethnic, psychological.

A perverse phenomenon is Jewish anti-Semitism, self-hatred and self-deprecation by Jews which is made evident in the books they write, movies they make and jokes they circulate.

Chapter 9

What Happens to the Jewish Partner?

I'm plagued with guilt. It must have been my fault that our daughter married a now-and-then-church-going Presbyterian, whose favorite day of the year is Christmas. Oh sure, Michelle attends High Holy Day services with us and is happy to help out with *seders* and family *Hanukkah* parties, but she could hardly be described as a committed Jew.

We're talking about our Michelle, who had her Torah Portion memorized two weeks before her *Bat Mitzvah* and was president of the temple youth group.

Where did we go wrong?

Ah, Jewish guilt, the stuff of which stand-up comedy routines, novels and films abound! If something has gone wrong, it must have been our fault. The truth is, we probably do much more that is right. That means you, too!

We would like to substitute caring for guilt. You have to care to feel guilt. You cared enough to make sure that Michelle had a *Bat Mitzvah,* and you must have been active enough in the temple so that Michelle was motivated to assume leadership in its youth group.

You probably did your best. It is possible, however, through no fault of yours, Michelle received an education in the rote and facade rather than the substance of Judaism.

Was the emphasis on memorizing the Torah Portion instead of understanding its significance? Was it on marching two or three steps to the left or right of the rabbi and cantor on the pulpit instead of applying Jewish ethics to behavior at home, school, camp or club?

Did the temple youth group concentrate on skating parties and pizza orgies, or were there also discussions about how to cope with the alienation and loneliness that plague teenagers, how to reach out to those who don't fit in?

Were there discussions about what it must have been like to have been a Jewish teenager in Inquisition Spain, in Russia during the pogroms, in Nazi Germany?

Were there discussions about the meaning of God and prayer and life?

Was there a huge "Bingo" sign on the synagogue facade, advertising it as an institution that benefitted financially from gambling, or was the synagogue a true sanctuary where one could be reflective and introspective?

Were the High Holy Days experienced as times of self-reflection and identity with every other Jew who ever lived, or were they fashion shows?

It's not too late! Michelle sounds as if she still wants to share Jewish experiences. How about suggesting that you and your daughter sign up for adult education classes on the role of women in Judaism or a course in Jewish ethics?

Maybe your son-in-law would enjoy the classes, too.

It's too easy to write off Jews like Michelle as being non-committed. We must concern ourselves, instead, with what it is to which they should be committed.

Our Ruthie, who had a Bat Mitzvah, was Confirmed, and even lived in Israel for a year, is now engaged to Wes, who says he agrees with the verse in one of his church's hymns, "I'm a Methodist 'till I die." He enjoys going to church a couple of Sundays a month, has a good friend who is a Methodist minister and gets as excited as a kid about his parents' Christmas celebrations.

Ruthie maintains she'll be able to live a Jewish life. Is that possible?

Yes, it is. Here are just some of the things Ruthie can choose to do:

- Attend synagogue services.

- Enroll in adult Jewish education classes.

- Subscribe to Jewish periodicals.

- Fight for the rights of Soviet Jews.

● Observe the Sabbath with prayer, reading or other relaxed activity.

Ruthie can do all these things and more. She is limited only by her interest and schedule. A Jew who marries a person who isn't remains a Jew.

Isn't it resentment on the part of the Jewish community toward intermarriages that has made continuing Jewish identity for the Jewish partners and their children in such marriages so difficult?

If this may have been true years ago, it is not so today. The current attitude of the Jewish community toward intermarriages can be described as one of trepidation rather than of resentment, because Jews fear the lessening of Jewish cohesiveness and the attrition in Jewish ranks.

The Jewish community wants desperately to retain the Jewish partner in an intermarriage and has designed "outreach" programs to do precisely that.

Can a Jew who is married to someone who isn't join a synagogue?

Yes. Orthodox and Conservative congregations, however, will not grant membership status to the non-Jewish husband or wife. Some Reform and Reconstructionist congregations will accept the non-Jewish husband or wife as a member but without voting status in the synagogue, while others will not grant membership to the non-Jewish spouse.

We raised our daughter in a good, Jewish home. But my friend, Irene, says that we must have done something wrong, or Abby wouldn't be marrying Eric. He is now enrolled in a conversion class. What do I tell Irene?

Put a lid on the judgment calls, Irene. Abby is devoted to her religion and loves it enough to introduce someone she loves to it. Eric's enrollment in a class for converts shows that he has shared positive Jewish experiences with Abby and the rest of your family. Now he wants total closeness and identification.

It is precious to present our religion to someone who was not born into it and have him adopt it as his own.

So, good night, Irene!

Leonard, our 27-year-old, has fallen in love, so he says, with a Jehovah's Witness. He maintains she has not tried to convert him, but we know that is just around the corner. How can we make him really "see the light"?

We have four suggestions. First, make your concern known in a straightforward but friendly manner. Second, do not lecture him every time you see him; it will only force him to find excuses to avoid being in your company. Third, recommend to Leonard that he attend church services with his friend and read up on her religion.

Fourth, Leonard should, in turn, urge her to attend synagogue services with him and read up on Judaism.

Won't that make Leonard more likely to consider conversion to her church?

Not unless he is looking to be seduced by a different religion. Since the suggestion comes from his Jewish parents, it will make it more of an objective experience.

Anyway, if they commit to a life together, he's going to find out plenty about her religion.

Encourage Leonard to ask pointed questions:

"Does your religion believe that you can be saved only if you believe in Jesus as the Christ?"

"Do the prayers of only born-again Christians reach God? What about the prayers of other Christians, Jews?"

"Does your faith teach you to seek converts urgently?"

After being exposed to each other's religions, Leonard and his friend might find themselves jarred at their mutual reactions and forced to rethink the prospects of a life together crammed with religious beliefs and practices that constantly are on a collision course.

Our daughter has married a young man who is a practicing Lutheran, and she has converted to that faith. She is like a stranger to us. Every time we visit her, we come home depressed. It is easier not to see her, but what will people think?

We understand your anguish. In earlier times, when civil marriages were almost unknown and marriage to a Christian almost always involved conversion to Christianity by the Jewish member of the couple, Jewish parents looked upon the apostate child as if he or she had died. Token mourning rituals were even held, and from that time forward the name of the son or daughter who had converted was never again mentioned in the Jewish family.

That was heartrending enough, but it was, in its grim way, a form of closure. Yours is a more difficult situation, assuming that you do not wish to break off the relationship with your daughter entirely.

"What will people think" is not at all the question. What do you want at this point in the relationship with your daughter, with her husband, with the grandchildren who have or who may come?

Perhaps, the best you may expect is a strained and cool relationship, but one in which you make it clear that you are still her mother and father, that you have never stopped loving her. The Hebrew Bible says that "love is as strong as death" *(Song of Songs, 8:6)*. It may be able to survive conversion from Judaism as well.

We raised our two sons with such strong Jewish commitment that Norm, our youngest, applied to and was accepted by a rabbinical seminary. In his senior year before ordination, a conversation he had with a young rabbi about the round-the-clock pressures of a congregational rabbi prompted Norm to shift gears and enter law school, instead.

Always a compassionate person, Norm is now in his second year of private practice, concentrating on environmental issues and involved in a law clinic which helps the poor and the elderly.

In the course of his work, Norma met an attorney who happens to be bright, beautiful and Episcopalian. Enter Maggie!

They were married by a judge two months ago and are now in the process of decorating their three-bedroom condo. The extra bedrooms are being used as private studies for each of them.

When Norm had his own apartment, he had on display in his living room an oil painting of a rabbi that he purchased

in Safed, Israel. Also in full view was his collection of more than 200 books of Jewish content.

The painting and the Jewish library are now stored in a closet in Norm's law office. When we asked him about this, Norm responded that he didn't want Maggie to feel that she had been thrust into an overwhelmingly Jewish environment.

How can we make our son understand that he is shielding his identity and that he may resent this in the future?

Has Maggie had anything to do with this concealment by Norm of the symbols of his Jewishness? Hadn't she noticed the painting and the books when she visited Norm's lodgings before they were married? If she had, and the presence of these Jewish items did not offend her, why the necessity for removing them from the new apartment?

You might want to ask these questions of Norm and, if possible, open up the matter of how he regards his Jewish identity now that he has married a woman who is not Jewish. What has happened, or will happen, when Christmas comes? Will there be a tree and other Yuletide decorations? Or, has there been a mutual agreement to keep the condo neutral of all sectarian symbolism?

It is truly tragic when intermarriage results in the need, real or fancied, for a cover-up of one's religious, ethnic or cultural identity. Such concealment puts a strain on the marriage tie and can lead to resentment which, added to the other, normal stresses in any marriage, may end up in bitterness and marital divisiveness.

My daughter-in-law, Gretchen, who isn't Jewish told the story of a woman at work who spent two years of her salary on a glitzy *Bar Mitzvah* for her son. Gretchen and my son attended the affair, which she described as "tacky and ostentatious." I feel this was an anti-Semitic comment.

Not at all. If you felt uncomfortable hearing her description of the bash, it was because you are honest and sensitive enough to know that her report was realistic.

Outrageously lavish *Bar Mitzvah* productions—the parties, not the services in synagogues—become a legitimate subject for derision by non-Jews as well as Jews. The feature pages of major metropolitan newspapers are replete with reports about the swarm of *Bar Mitzvah* spectaculars that compete for hedonistic honors.

A New York Jets guard was the featured speaker at one of these posh extravaganzas held in a huge football stadium in the East. What a moment in Jewish history it was when a high school band marched in formation to etch across the huge field the name of the *Bar Mitzvah* lad!

Segue to a shipboard *Bar Mitzvah* on the QE2. As the luxurious liner steamed out of New York Harbor, a crew of 1,000 attended to the needs of the 600 guests who feted the *Bar Mitzvah* celebrant as they ate, swam and gambled.

When Jews stop skyrocketing the expenditures in order to keep up with the Cohens in producing *Bar* and *Bat Mitzvah* orgies and, instead, share their *simcha* (joyous event) with the needy, we all will feel more comfortable.

I know it would have been best had my daughter and son-in-law talked more about religion before their marriage, but they didn't. They live 2,000 miles away from us, close to his parents, which brings me to the problem. His parents have been very active in the local Unitarian church. They are always inviting Shana and Bret to church socials and services. The church has a very active social action program.

Everyone there is friendly. Shana calls and tells us that although they are in a big city they feel as if they belong to a large, extended family.

There's no pressure to contribute money, although donations are requested. And it's stipulated that wealth cannot buy honors in the church; only volunteer service does that.

At Shana's request, she and Bret checked out the local synagogue. Shana described the persons she met there as cold and tending to stick with people they already knew.

Because Shana had requested that she be placed on the mailing list, she and Bret were contacted about membership in the temple. They are both teachers in their late 20s and couldn't believe the amount of money for which they were being asked. They were told that if there was some sort of financial problem, they could bring in their federal income tax returns for the previous year for an evaluation of any "special circumstances" there might be.

You might have guessed the outcome. Shana and Bret returned to the Unitarian congregation. Our daughter says that she still considers herself Jewish, but it is this church that is filling her needs for companionship and involvement. And there is no financial pressure.

What can be done about this?

This is a truly sad story you have brought before us, sad not only for your daughter and son-in-law, but sad for members of the synagogue they visited who probably need and want the warmth, involvement and feeling of belonging that the church members apparently receive.

Ironically, all of the needs you described can be filled by practicing the basic tenets of Judaism itself. When newcomers find themselves within a Jewish environment, the Biblical imperative of "Remember the stranger; for you, too, were strangers in the land of Egypt" should immediately become operative. When a Jewish person seeks a synagogue or Jewish center to alleviate strong feelings of alienation and loneliness, the post-Biblical advice to "acquire a friend" should be extended at once to him or to her.

Institutionalized Judaism in the United States, especially the synagogue, is in a critical phase. Its leadership knows it but acts as if it is paralyzed.

The problem is that American synagogues in many cases have become corporate entities in which only upper middle class families can find themselves comfortable. Huge budgets are called for in the operation of impressive physical plants—the so-called Edifice Complex—with a professional staff of rabbis, cantors, Jewish educators, temple administrators, as well as clerical and maintenance personnel.

The weekday Hebrew school conducted by almost all congregations is highly professionalized, as it should be, and is a major "loss leader," to use a marketing term, which results in a tremendous drain.

What do do? There is an urgent need to reassess the operational core of the synagogue. A classic instance is the costly operation of Jewish religious schools which we have mentioned. On the surface, it is simple to say that congregations should not maintain duplicative educational establishments and that, instead, the organized Jewish community should take over the operation of Hebrew and day schools.

Simple to state, but, in the minds of the congregation leadership, it would be a fatal move. Since many—some would say most—U.S. Jews affiliate with a synagogue, at the beginning certainly, because they want to take advantage of the congregation's educational services for their children, where would the synagogue be if it no longer maintained its own school?

A proposal was made many decades ago by the late Rabbi Mordecai M. Kaplan, founder of the Jewish Reconstructionist movement, that we should have what he termed "organic" Jewish communities in this country. Jews would voluntarily affiliate and pay taxes to the organized, organic Jewish community which, in turn, would centralize fund-raising, maintain houses of worship and religious schools, engage and pay rabbis, cantors, educators and other functionaries.

This was the *Kehilla* plan, which operated successfully for many decades in certain European Jewish communities. When Dr. Kapaln attempted to adapt it to the huge New York Jewish community, it perished aborning.

Meanwhile, your daughter, Shana, and who knows how many other hundreds of thousands of young and older single Jews and couples, find themselves excluded from the organized Jewish community and wide open to the warm, nurturing embraces of legitimate churches as well as cults.

During the Holocaust, there was a Yiddish song called *"Es brennt,"* which told of a Jewish village in flames, while Jews stood around, helplessly, incapable of dousing the fire. To a critical extent, this can be said of our Jewish establishment in the United States. When synagogue leadership has budget and edifice tunnel-vision, the precious values of Judaism are lost.

Here's an idea for Shana: She should sit down and write the rabbi and the president of the temple where she had the experience which turned her off. As in other instances, silence, or leaving the job for others to do, simply contributes to the malaise.

Please ask Shana to try other synagogues. Many provide warm, caring environments where she can share the wonder that is Judaism.

What do you mean by "the wonder that is Judaism"? If I don't understand it myself, how can I convey it to Shana?

The history of the Jews has been described as the Romance of a People, and the only meaningful relationship a Jew, by birth or conversion, can have with Judaism is to fall in love with it! So much of our time and energy is spent in Jewish organizational activity and so little in Jewish living that we forget to "romance" our Judaism. If we paid more attention to what the Jewish essence is, we would have far less confusion about the value of perpetuating it.

Let's get down to the nitty-gritty. At the very minimum, we are describing a faith and its way of life that recognize your uniqueness. Recognition begins with a ceremony welcoming you into the world (baby-naming or *b'rit milah)* and ushers you out of this life with dignity in a format of mourning that takes people through the stages of grief when they lose a loved one.

The Jewish essence emphasizes, among other things, accepting yourself, loving yourself. Our great teacher, Hillel, put it succinctly, "If I am not for myself, who will be for me?" He followed it immediately with "If I am for myself alone, what am I?" The Ba'al Shem Tov, founder of Hassidism, made it clear that the meaning of the Jewish teaching, "You shall love your neighbor as yourself"—which, by the way, preceded Christianity's Golden Rule—is that before you can love another of God's creatures you must be able to love yourself.

God's creatures, indeed. Judaism first established the concept of monotheism in the world, that there is One God and one only, to challenge the false gods that people worship even today.

Never forget that Judaism functions as the connective tissue of your life; that is, it connects us with the generations that have gone before and with those that will follow. It warns you not to alienate yourself. "Don't separate yourself from the community," the Talmud cautions.

How is all this accomplished? By a richness of delights: Torah, teaching the oral and written Law, by rituals and symbols, by the Sabbath, holy days and festivals.

Take a refresher look at *Shabbat,* the Sabbath. It provides respite from the high tech, computer-oriented world of the marketplace, and opportunity to withdraw and study, meditate, pray, enjoy the ballet or opera, take dinner with friends and family. The Sabbath becomes a sanctuary for the soul, a celebration of the week that has passed and of the promise that lies in the week to come.

Perhaps you crave an opportunity for introspection in this age of anxiety and stress. Judaism affords *Rosh Hashanah,* the New Year, and *Yom Kippur,* the Day of Atonement, to take annual inventory of attitudes and deeds, to examine who you are, where you came from and where you're heading.

Here, again Judaism becomes the "connective tissue," because the sounds of the *shofar* which awaken you are the same sounds that have stirred Jews for thousands of years. Even as the haunting melody of *Kol Nidre* moves you deeply, you are thrilled by the awareness that around the planet, in cities and their suburbs, on ships at sea, Jews are stirred as you are to confession of sins.

It is Judaism that reminds you to lift your eyes away from the freeways and turnpikes, from the concrete canyons, from polluted skies and presents you with *Shavuot* and *Sukkot* festivals to remember the spring and autumn harvests, a *Tu B'Shvat* holiday to remind you of trees, and Passover and *Hanukkah* to recall that you cannot take freedom for granted.

Yours is a life-affirming faith that tells you to celebrate your zest for living, *l'Hayyim,* that teaches sensitivity to the environment and to animals who share our world.

Jews do believe that God works in and through history, and Jewish history is resplendent with a passion for freedom and for justice. One prophet of Israel cries out, "Justice, Justice shall you pursue!" while another declares, "What does God want of you? Only to do justice, to love mercy!"

If someone should ask you what Judaism has to offer, the answer is: dignity, compassion, the power of positive thinking, a sense of community, meditation, prayer, scholarship, ritual, symbolism, spiritual fulfillment, mysticism, rationality—as much or as little of any or all of these for which you may yearn.

When we are lonely and afraid, when our hurts are so profound that we fear they may never heal, Judaism is there to cloak us, comfort us, nurture us with the skill of a faith that has weathered the millenia and seen Jews through the best of times and the worst of times.

Tell Shana that nothing can take the real, the genuine, the authentic Judaism away from her, not the Bingo signs that foul the sanctuary grounds, not the people talking during the service, neither an occasional pretentious rabbi, strutting cantor nor a swaggering temple official—none can take Judaism, authentic Judaism, away from her.

Martin Buber, one of the greatest Jewish thinkers of all times, described it as the "I-THOU" relationship, that simple yet elegant empathy with all that is positive in the universe; with God, the Power that makes for good within us, and with eternity.

Most important, please remind Shana that it is her choice to turn her back on Judaism, but—and it is a big BUT—it is also her responsibility to understand what she is leaving behind.

Chapter 10

"Till Death Us Do Part"

If my child intermarries, who will say *Kaddish* for me when I am gone?

Those whom you ask while you are alive. Explain to them that Judaism provides an unique structure for coping with death. There are ceremonies of closure to commemorate our lives, kindle memories and comfort the bereaved. This format recognizes the need for social and personal mourning and for dealing with guilt.

Explain to your children and grandchildren your desire for the *Kaddish* to be said after you have passed on. If they are old enough to understand, they will be grateful that you have provided them with a tangible way of honoring your life.

Failure to honor the memory of a deceased parent and neglecting to observe the Jewish laws of mourning, including the saying of *Kaddish*, is not limited to families where intermarriage has occurred but is, unfortunately, endemic among Jews, intermarried or not.

I recently attended the funeral service for a colleague who retired several years ago. She was a widow whose two children had both been intermarried, The son and daughter attended the service with their respective children, who bore such typically unJewish names as Christopher and Margaret.

A rabbi was called upon to conduct the service; however, he was requested not to use any Hebrew, because nobody would understand him.

I was actually a witness to the last rites for Judaism in this family.

I am especially troubled, because my daughter is engaged to a man who isn't Jewish. Ever since my friend's funeral, I've been having nightmares about my own funeral service being conducted without the Hebrew prayers and witnessed by grandchildren who aren't Jewish.

Every adult, especially of advancing years, should prepare an informal document detailing what kind of a funeral ceremony he or she desires. It should include all the necessary specifics about the place where the funeral or memorial service is to be held, the type of casket, the garment in which you wish to be buried, where the remains are to be interred, or scattered in the case of a cremation.

Included, also, should be the very important instructions about who should conduct the funeral liturgy, who deliver the eulogy or eulogies, as well as the specific nature of the prayers, other readings and music you would like to have included in the service.

These instructions should be left in a readily accessible place, known to persons closest to you. If you are up to it emotionally, it is a good idea to go over the content of the instructions with the person or persons who will be responsible for carrying them out.

If this had been done in the instance of your friend, the problems which occurred in connection with her last rites could have been avoided.

The lack of Jewish identity of your grandchildren should not be of concern to you when you think about your last rites. God willing, they will be people you have loved and who will have loved you throughout your long life, to the very end.

May a husband or wife who isn't Jewish be buried next to his or her Jewish spouse in a Jewish cemetery?

Yes, but not with a Christian religious interment service or with the liturgical participation of a Christian clergyperson.

This holds true for modern Jewish burial grounds. Older Jewish cemeteries, if chartered by Orthodox synagogues, may have prohibitions against the burial of non-Jews, spouses or otherwise, in their rules and regulations.

In the event of the death at the same time of an intermarried couple, may a rabbi and a member of the Christian clergy co-officiate at the funeral?

In theory, yes, at least so far as the Reform or Reconstructionist denominations are concerned. However, the obstacles can be so overwhelming that the theory is lost in the shuffle.

Assuming that the funeral rites, or, at least, the interment would take place in a Jewish cemetery rather than in a non-denominational one, be aware that Jewish burial grounds would not permit the participation of non-Jewish clergy without a rabbi or the inclusion of a non-Jewish funeral liturgy. If a non-Jewish clergyperson were to join a rabbi in the service, his or her reading would have to be non-sectarian or, at the very least, drawn from the "old" Testament.

A rabbi would find it virtually impossible to officiate in a non-Jewish cemetery in the presence of a Christian colleague who invoked the Trinity and read from a Protestant or Roman Catholic funeral ritual which was filled with Christological references.

We can well understand that these details and restrictions may distress you. May we suggest a compromise that will avoid any conflicts? Hold a memorial service on "neutral" territory, such as a home, instead of an interment service in the Jewish cemetery. This would do away with any problem of a rabbi and a Christian clergyperson taking part.

Chapter 11

Jews by Choice

Is marriage between a Jew and a convert to Judaism a Jewish marriage?

Of course it is. That's like asking whether a marriage between two Jews is a Jewish marriage. Once converted to Judaism, the person is a Jew.

How can we urge conversion?

That's not fair. It would be wrong for someone to convert to Judaism just to please someone else.

Before taking even the initial steps, candidates for conversion have many things to consider, among them commitment to their parents' religion, desire to retain identification with their own memories.

Judaism wants sincere converts.

What can be urged is a familiarity with Judaism. When you love someone, you should know about his or her background. That means not only the cute pictures and films of the beloved as a romping toddler but also learning about the ancestral heritage—and the religious, ethnic and cultural environment.

What happens in a class for prospective converts?

For several months, potential converts read and discuss Jewish history, beliefs, holidays and practices. They learn how Judaism differs from Christianity and other religions. Field trips to synagogues are scheduled to familiarize the students with Jewish religions symbols and services.

In Orthodox and Conservative Judaism, the course of study is followed by a ceremony of immersion in water and, for a man, ritual circumcision, a token procedure if the man is already circumcised. Some Reform rabbis do not require immersion and circumcision.

Now comes the formal conversion ceremony before three witnesses, usually rabbis, during which the convert is asked to disclaim his or her former religious beliefs and to recite the *Shema,* the Hebrew announcement of belief in One God. *(Deuteronomy 6:4).*

The convert is given a Hebrew name in addition to his or her given English name. For example, a woman might receive the name of Ruth, "the daughter of Abraham our father and Sara our mother," thereby linking her to the beginnings of Jewish history.

The conversion ceremony may take place in a rabbi's study or on a synagogue pulpit.

That's it; no mystery, no pressure.

Do you mean that there's no pressure to convert?

That's right. In Judaism, the conversion process is totally free of duress or any kind of emotional intimidation. While studying, an individual makes no advance commitment. The decision to convert must come voluntarily.

My future son-in-law is a very successful plumbing contractor and is interested in converting to Judaism. He says he never has been a good student; he just isn't one of those guys who can hit the books. Do you have to be a good student to succeed in a conversion class? Are there exams and papers to write?

Tell him not to worry. Introduction to Judaism courses for potential converts are not academic in nature. Students are asked to show good faith and interest, not the ability to memorize and regurgitate information. He'll be happy to know there are no grades, no research papers, no exams. Sometimes, students are asked to write reports. He can get help with these from your daughter, who will be asked to take the class with him. Or, he might work out an alternative assignment with the instructor.

Your son-in-law to-be will do fine, and we're happy to have him aboard!

How does someone convert to Jewish ethnicity?

You have touched upon a raw nerve! Conversion to Judaism is not the single act of affirmation of a creed, as in Christianity, but becoming a member of a minority which has had a long history of being victimized, discriminated against and subjected to bodily harm. It is difficult for a person born and reared in a majority Christian culture to accept the history of the Jewish people as his or her personal history and to identify with Jewish aspirations and anxieties.

What is ethnicity? It is the in-group feeling of those who share a common culture or religion or language or national origin.

What is Jewish ethnicity? For the person who was not born into it, it can be the challenge of being in a self-segregating Jewish environment with its nuances and overtones, spiced with American Yiddishisms that cause Jews to react with chuckles and belly laughs, while the outsider becomes a passive spectator with a fixed smile.

It can be the ethnicity to be found in a *Kosher* or "Kosher-style" deli, crowded during the lunch hour on weekdays with Jewish business men and women or, on a Saturday or Sunday night, with exuberant and boisterous Jewish couples and families.

On a somber note, ethnicity can be the sensitivity of Jews to neo-Nazi parades, anti-Semitism, graffiti and vandalism, and evocations of the Holocaust.

Despite this, many converts to Judaism, especially those who made their commitment for reasons other than expediency, become ethnic Jews. They take seriously the fact that they have thrown their lot in with the Jewish people and, like Ruth in the Biblical story, sincerely believe that "your people shall be my people and your God my God."

You can find such adoptive Jews playing creative and significant roles in Jewish communal life.

Don't many converts know a lot more about Judaism than persons who are born Jewish?

Without a doubt. Converts learn about Judaism as adults. They can appreciate the romance of Jewish history and the relevance of Jewish ideas. Too many people who are born Jewish dabble in a smattering of Bible stories and Hebrew lessons when they are kids, only to drop the whole thing after the *Bar* or *Bat Mitzvah* party; and they never find out what teriffic stuff they're missing.

Hasn't conversion always been a survival tool for Jews by keeping the numbers from plummeting?

Not really. When the number of Jews in the world might have been affected by killings in the Spanish Inquisition or pogroms in Eastern Europe, the very nature of these attacks made conversion to Judaism and affiliation with the Jewish people somewhat less than appealing.

Traditionally, Judaism viewed proselytizing for converts with less than enthusiasm. Jews have never wanted to accept converts who came to us under conditions of duress or because of expediency; for example, with the sole intent of marrying a Jew.

In the changed conditions of our times, converts are welcomed much more enthusiastically, provided they seek admission to Judaism of their own free will. Each year, thousands of converts are accepted and welcomed into Judaism.

Their addition does help to add to the ranks of the Jewish people which have been decimated by the slaughter of six million Jews during the Holocaust in addition to those lost through assimilation.

When our son, Bradley, asked Joan to marry him four years ago, he also asked her to convert to Judaism. Joan explained that while her ties to the church in which she was raised were nominal she did not want to sever them. She told Bradley that she loved him, but she would not convert. They were married.

Now, they want to start a family, and Bradley is urging Joan to convert, so that the children can be raised in a total Jewish environment. We agree with him. But Joan remains stubborn. What can we do?

Lay off! It's not fair that Bradley demanded that Joan convert now, since he married her despite her open refusal to become Jewish. And it's super unfair that you team up with him to pressure her.

My daughter's fiance, Greg, says that he would convert to Judaism, but it would upset his teen-age daughter from a previous marriage. My daughter feels that his first loyalty should be to their forthcoming marriage. I agree with her. How can we make Greg see this?

We have already indicated that conversion under duress is frowned upon in Judaism. However, if Greg is truly receptive to the idea of becoming Jewish, the wishes of his daughter should not be relevant. Greg's concern over his daughter's feelings in matters concerning his new marriage may be symptomatic of a deeper problem, both on his part as well as his daughter's.

My daughter tells me that she knows women who convert to Judaism to make sure they snare Jewish men who will not marry them otherwise. The commitment of these women to Judaism is zero, and nothing real is communicated to their children.
Is marrying a non-Jew worse than this?

Judaism has always looked askance upon any form of conversion for convenience. That includes a phony conversion to grease the path toward marriage or to please the parents of the Jewish partner.

In such an instance, you are correct. It is better to recognize a mixed marriage as just that rather than go through the choreography of an insincere conversion.

Isn't it best to convert after the marriage, when the person has a chance to live as a Jew for a while and is exposed to the synagogue and the Jewish family?

The problem is that, in most cases, the marriage ceremony will not be a Jewish one, which sort of puts a kind of sour note on future plans for conversion. Anyhow, except in instances of hurry-up weddings, most people marry after a period of getting to know each other in all areas, including, very often, living together.

My daughter, Laura, is engaged to Spence, a widower with a 5-year-old son, Blake. Spence was raised a Methodist but lost interest in the denomination years ago. Blake hasn't been exposed to any religious experience except for tree-trimming and gift-giving Christmas celebrations.

Spence intends to convert to Judaism before the wedding. How can Blake be converted to Judaism? Is it fair to make that choice for a child? Blake's maternal grandparents say that the idea is outrageous. Laura adores Blake and is concerned about erasing the memory of his mother, who died when Blake was 2 years old.

You present several provocative questions. First, let's deal with the objection raised by the parents of Blake's late mother. The determination of a child's welfare, religious or otherwise, is the prerogative of his or her parents and not that of the grandparents, aunts, uncles or anyone else. Since Blake's mother is deceased, Spence alone has the right to make the choices for his child.

If Spence wants it, Blake should be reared as a Jew, given a good Jewish education—day school or week-day Hebrew school, plus reputable Jewish summer camp—including *Bar Mitzvah* and Confirmation.

You ask how Blake can be converted to Judaism. Since he will have been reared as a Jew from early childhood, no formal conversion procedure would be required in the Reform and Reconstructionist denominations. For Orthodox or Conservative conversion, Blake will have to go through ritual immersion and circumcision under anesthesia, if he is not already circumcised.

So far as Laura's concern that Blake should not forget his natural mother, this can be solved by keeping photographs of his real mother in Blake's room as well as speaking about her as he matures.

I converted to Judaism 30 years ago, when I married Seth. We have been blessed with a fine marriage and three children, two daughters and our son, David.

When I met Seth, I was touched by the warmth that his family showed me. Three decades ago, it was very frightening to bring home a non-Jewish woman, but Seth's parents, who were very active in their Reform synagogue, were kind and gracious. They invited me to all their Jewish holiday celebrations even before we became engaged.

One day, I helped my future mother-in-law rescue a stray

dog; and we both realized that we had a lot in common and would be close friends, which we were until her passing six years ago.

I loved Seth. I loved his family. And I learned to love Judaism. My family was very close-knit but not religious. As a matter of fact, when I announced to my parents that I was going to convert to Judaism, they were actually pleased that I had on my own found a meaningful religion.

Now, our son, David, who is 26, has found someone he loves very much. Rayna is a bouncy, bubbly, warm 25-year-old Jewish woman. Her parents claim that David isn't really Jewish, because I was converted by a Reform rabbi. They say David's not a true Jew. If he is going to marry their Rayna, they maintain he will have to go through conversion under Orthodox auspices.

I never imagined I could be so hurt. What can we do?

Orthodox rabbis do not accept as religiously valid conversions performed under the supervision of non-Orthodox rabbis. The refusal of Orthodox Judaism both on the American continent and in the State of Israel to recognize conversions to Judaism that were not performed by Orthodox rabbis has catapulted the "Who is a Jew?" question to the forefront of today's religious agenda.

If Rayna loves David, the two of them will have to assert their unwillingness to have their nuptials subjected to religious nit-picking. With all due respect to those who differ, David is Jewish. He should not and must not be viewed or treated as an interloper.

One caveat: you and your husband should be supportive but not enter the fray. David and Rayna are old enough and, presumably, mature enough to state and hold fast to their position. You and they should know that the overwhelming majority of American Jews are on David's side.

Chapter 12

Uncle Louie
and
Uncle Oscar

We have a problem of name-calling in our family. When we have our Cousins' Club picnic each summer, Uncle Louis attends with his children, who are my first cousins. As soon as he spies my non-Jewish daughter-in-law, Lorna, whom I adore, he shouts out from wherever he is standing or sitting, "Hey, kid! How's my little *shiksah?*"

If I've asked Uncle Louie once, I've asked him a dozen times to stop calling Lorna a *shiksah*. He only laughs and tells me that she loves it. I'm embarrassed, and I apologize to Lorna every time it happens. She says it's no problem, but I know she is uncomfortable about it. My son says what can you expect from a slob like Uncle Louie, but that doesn't solve anything.

In its origin, the word, *shiksah,* is both Hebrew as well as Yiddish, the vernacular of Jews in pre-Holocaust Eastern Europe. It refers to a non-Jewish woman or girl. The Yiddish word for a non-Jewish man or boy is *shaygitz*. Neither of these words is in itself disparaging. Like any names, however, the question of whether they are pejorative has to be determined by the context in which they are used.

Uncle Louie ought to be told in explicit terms, since we gather that he is not one for subtleties, to cease and desist from referring to Lorna as a *shiksah*. Further, uncle should be informed that the next time he flaps his jaws and spits out the word, he will publicly be called a *shmuck*. The person to tell Louie off is your son. It's about time he did something to protect his Lorna's feelings rather than continuing to act like a *shlemiehl*.

Oscar is the patriarch of our family. He's my husband's elder brother, a tall, heavyset man who's made a killing in discount household appliances. His wife, Dot—formerly Dora—is a short, pudgy ball of fire who thinks nothing of inviting 27 relatives to dinner on short notice in honor of an out-of-town cousin who just dropped in and can only stay for two days.

Oscar and Dottie host several lavish family gatherings each year, organize family junkets to their four-bedroom, mountain lakeside retreat and present a major appliance—refrigerator, dishwasher or washer and dryer—to each child of a family member who marries.

The only members of the family who are included out of the galas are my daughter, Beverly; her Gentile husband, Doug, and their 6-year-old son, Shepherd. Oscar has ruled that anyone who marries a non-Jew is to be banned from the family's social circle.

Beverly has more Jewish connections than almost anyone else in the family. She attends temple services on the average of a couple of times a month, usually accompanied by Doug. Their son is enrolled in the first grade of the synagogue Sunday School.

Beverly is active in a Jewish feminist group, contributes money to a shelter for battered women in Israel and to the Israel Society for the Prevention of Cruelty to Animals, writes letters to legislators on behalf of Soviet Jewry, reads Jewish books and takes an adult education course at the temple.

Doug not only supports our daughter's Jewish activities and approves of having Shepherd raised as a Jew but has used his skills as an attorney on behalf of Jewish causes. Just the other day, he was the first caller to a radio station to protest its playing of an old Irish folk song about a Jewish moneylender.

Back to Oscar and Dottie. They rarely attend synagogue services. The last time in the past 12 months was on *Rosh Hashanah*. At that time, Oscar prayed downstairs with the men, while Dottie craned her neck to see her husband from her perch in the women's gallery upstairs. She was to watch for a signal from Oscar, a wave of his *tallit*, that would alert her that the time had come to leave for home ahead of him to prepare the holiday dinner.

"If you're going to *shule*, you go Orthodox; it's the only way," pontificates Oscar, who never returned for the *Yom*

Kippur service, because he and Dottie were leaving on a Caribbean cruise.

This year, when he attended a Passover *seder* sponsored by his country club, Oscar was irate. It seems that the rabbi who had been engaged by the club to conduct the *seder* tied the story of the Hebrew slaves in Egypt to the plight of migrant farm workers in the United States.

"Why didn't he stick to Judaism?" Oscar grumbled over the phone as he described the event to us. "And they didn't even put enough *matza* balls in the soup. Some *seder!*"

His rancor escalated when he and Dottie attended a *Bar Mitzvah* at a Reform temple. "Imagine! The men's heads were uncovered! Women held the *Torah!* They even had a female cantor! You call that Judaism?" he snorted at a family dinner. "But I showed them. I pushed away the usher's hand when he tried to give me a prayer book. You won't catch me praying in a Jewish church!"

Our Beverly doesn't care about the kitchen appliances she didn't get when Oscar and Dottie boycotted her wedding to Doug; but she does miss the family connection. Most of the family's social life is held under the auspices of Oscar and Dot.

What can be done about this predicament?

Our sympathy! Your family has the misfortune of having in its midst a NOOJ. NOOJ is our acronym for Non-Observant Orthodox Jew. Oscar fits the description to a T, and we don't mean *tallit* or *tefillin*. Like every other NOOJ, Oscar is self-righteous, judgmental and consistently hypocritical.

Defining a NOOJ like Oscar is easier than solving the problem he presents. In the long run, Beverly, Doug and, most of all, young Shepherd will be better off having the least amount of contact with a perverse individual like Oscar and his long-suffering spouse, Dottie. She, by the way, fits the definition of the word.

Why are you, your husband and Beverly and her husband so dependent on Uncle Oscar? Don't you make yourselves appear to be mendicants, subservient to his cruel indulgences and petty prejudices, while you wait to be welcomed to the festive table by a nod of his scepter?

What about Oscar's younger brother, your husband? He seems to operate on the assumption that he must stand by like a wimp in deference to his senior sibling, while Oscar humiliates Beverly, her husband and their child. Isn't it time for some brotherly frankness?

As each one of us must, when hapless enough to be in the presence of a NOOJ, you must assert your independence. Begin to hold your own family parties for the holidays and on birthday and anniversary occasions and by so doing demonstrate that you and your husband, or Beverly and Doug, can be hosts of gatherings that make up in fun and a genial atmosphere what they might lack in Oscar's bluster.

Courteously but firmly nudge your resident NOOJ into a harmless corner of your family life.

Appendix

The Intermarriage
Prenuptial Pact

Our daughter, Anita, is engaged to Jim, who is not Jewish. Is there anything they can do to prepare themselves to cope with the challenges that will face them in their intermarriage?

We recommend an intermarriage prenuptial pact. The concept of prenuptial pacts worked out and mutually agreed upon by couples who are planning marriage and who have individual financial holdings has become increasingly popular and effective. The pact we have formulated is suitable for insuring vital communication that can help stave off problems arising from an intermarriage. It can also be adopted as a legal agreement. Please show this to Anita and Jim!

The first step is to gather background information. This is going to be fun, because you're going to find out so much about each other. As you share memories, feelings and hopes, you will also be taking a religious inventory of your lives that will help you make crucial decisions about the future the two of you will share. The process could take days, possibly weeks.

Explore your individual religious upbringing. Did you have a ritual circumcision? A christening? Were you baptized? Did you attend Sunday school, Hebrew school, parochial school? Did you win awards for regular attendance at religious school? Did you have a *Bar Mitzvah* or a *Bat Mitzvah?* Did you make your First Communion? Were you Confirmed? Would you want your children to have these experiences?

Which religious holidays are most memorable for you? Reminisce about special moments on the Sabbath, at *Rosh Hashanah, Yom Kippur,* Passover, Christmas and Easter.

Discuss the roles religion has played in your respective lives. Do you believe in God? What is your concept of God? Do you believe in Jesus? Do you feel that your religion has given you strength, identity, an ethical frame of reference with which to relate to the world? Have you had a special relationship with a rabbi, priest, minister, nun or guru? How did this person influence your life?

How does religion fit into the lives of your parents? Young people so often struggle to break away from their parents' life styles that it is difficult for them to assimilate the idea that all of us emulate our parents to some degree. Our parents are our first role models. Their habits, mannerisms, speech patterns and attitudes are programmed in our heads. We can't tell you the number of times we have heard middle-aged persons comment about their spouses, "He turned into his father." "I close my eyes and hear her mother."

Do you own religious art, music, books, a *mezuzah,* crucifix, a nativity creche, special Christmas tree ornaments, a *menorah, Kiddush* cup, Sabbath candlesticks? Do you treasure these?

Is one of you committed to converting to the religion of the other? We emphasize the seriousness of this step. The decision can be a traumatic one, charged with emotions that include feelings of rejection on the part of your immediate family members. It must come out of a profound understanding of and commitment to the adoptive religion.

Now, with your religious inventory on the table, you are ready to draft your INTERMARRIAGE PRENUPTIAL PACT.

1. RELIGIOUS IDENTITY

Pledge that if each of you has decided to keep his or her own religious identity without conversion, there will be no pressure brought to bear after the marriage to convert. You must refrain from pressuring your spouse to make a commitment to your own religion. Each spouse will be allowed to maintain and express his or her religious convictions.

2. HOME ENVIRONMENT

Determine whether there will be religious symbols in the home. Will a *mezuzah* greet visitors as they approach the doorpost of your home? Will a religious medallion rest on a nightstand? Will a crucifix hang over the bed in the master bedroom or the guest room? Will paintings and posters with religious themes be hung over the mantel or the sofa or in the foyer? Will religious books be on conspicuous display?

3. HOLIDAYS

Will each of you attend religious services in observance of the Jewish or Christian Sabbaths, *Rosh Hashanah, Yom Kippur,* Passover, Christmas, Easter or various saints' days?

Will the Sabbath, *Hanukkah,* Passover, Christmas and Easter be celebrated in the home? Will there be Sabbath candles, a *menorah,* "Happy *Hanukkah"* banners, a Christmas tree, Christmas angels, lights, a nativity creche, a wreath on the door? Will you send Jewish New Year cards to family and friends? Will you send out Christmas cards? Will you go caroling?

4. CHILDREN

Will your children have a religious identity? Will there be a naming in the synagogue when a baby girl arrives, a ritual circumcision for a boy, a baptism or christening?

Will your children receive religious instruction? Which religious holidays will the kids celebrate? How about Santa Claus and the Easter Bunny? Will the children attend a church or a synagogue school?

In the event both of you die while the children are young, who will have custody? Who will be charged with their religious upbringing?

Should your marriage end in divorce, how will the religious identity of your children be handled, if one parent retains custody?

5. RESIDENCE

Determine the type of neighborhood in which you would like to reside. One partner may want to live amid a concentration of people who share his or her ethnic and religious affiliation. Will the other spouse be comfortable in that environment?

6. FINANCES

Determine whether a portion of the family's financial resources will be contributed toward the support of a synagogue or church, religious schools, religious social services agencies and overseas missionary or philanthropic organizations, the State of Israel support groups.

7. DEATH

Specify the type of funeral services you would like for yourself; if religious, what denomination?

Would you want a clergyperson to officiate? Of what faith?

What traditions would you like incorporated into the service? Which mourning practices would you like to be followed?

Do you want to be interred in a cemetery which is Jewish, Christian or non-sectarian? Since your spouse is of another faith, do you want to be buried next to him or her in the same cemetery, when the time comes?

A CLOSING THOUGHT

Any kind of prenuptial agreement sounds forbidding, at the very least very unromantic. As we have pointed out, however, such an agreement in connection with an intermarriage affords both parties a real opportunity to explore, in what should be a relaxed mood, areas that, after marriage, could conceivably become points of tension and contention.

JACOBS LADDER PUBLICATIONS

CLUES ABOUT JEWS FOR PEOPLE WHO AREN'T, by Sidney J. Jacobs and Betty J. Jacobs. $8.95. A lively, information-packed guide to understanding and getting along with Jewish friends, business associates, neighbors and relatives. This gutsy volume answers 201 questions people who aren't Jewish typically ask about those who are.

"Compassionate and insightful . . . gently debunks many of the stereotypes about the Jewish people."　　　　*Los Angeles Times*

"An excellent book."　　　　*National Jewish Post and Opinion*

"This is one of the most useful little books I have ever encountered."
Jewish News of Essex County

"For Jews by birth and Jews by choice, for families of folks who have married Jews and for other interested non-Jews, these clues will amuse, inform and satisfy curiosity. Besides they make good reading."

United Synagogue Review

Order through better bookstores, or send $8.95 plus $1.50 shipping and handling to JACOBS LADDER PUBLICATIONS Box 1484 Culver City, California 90232.

122 Clues For Jews
Whose Children Intermarry
has been set in 10 point Century Schoolbook
and printed on 70 lb. Simpson Opaque Vellum at
Peace Press, Los Angeles, California

Design by Pam Apostolou
Typesetting by Freddie Hart